FOUNDATIONS OF MODERN ECONOMICS SERIES

Otto Eckstein, *Editor*

American Industry: Structure, Conduct, Performance, 3rd Ed., *Richard Caves*
Prices and Markets, 2nd Ed., *Robert Dorfman*
The Price System, *Robert Dorfman*
Money and Credit: Impact and Control, 3rd Ed., *James S. Duesenberry*
Public Finance, 3rd Ed., *Otto Eckstein*
Economies and the Environment, *Matthew Edel*
Managerial Economics, *Farrar and Meyer*
Labor Economics, *Richard B. Freeman*
Economic Development: Past and Present, 3rd Ed., *Richard T. Gill*
Evolution of Modern Economics, *Richard T. Gill*
Economic Systems, *Gregory Grossman*
Student Guide, *Hartman and Gustafson*
International Economics, 3rd Ed., *Kenan and Lubitz*
National Income Analysis, 3rd Ed., *Charles L. Schultze*

FOUNDATIONS OF MODERN ECONOMICS SERIES

JAMES S. DUESENBERRY *Harvard University*

Money and Credit: Impact and Control

THIRD EDITION

PRENTICE-HALL, INC. *Englewood Cliffs, New Jersey*

ISBN: P-0-13-600304-4

ISBN: C-0-13-600312-5

Library of Congress Catalog Number 70-173310

PRENTICE-HALL FOUNDATIONS OF MODERN ECONOMICS SERIES

Otto Eckstein, *Editor*

10 9 8 7 6 5 4 3 2

PRENTICE-HALL INTERNATIONAL INC., *London*
PRENTICE-HALL OF AUSTRALIA, PTY., LTD., *Sydney*
PRENTICE-HALL OF CANADA, LTD., *Toronto*
PRENTICE-HALL OF INDIA PVT. LIMITED, *New Delhi*
PRENTICE-HALL OF JAPAN, INC., *Tokyo*

Contents

Foundations of Modern Economics Series

Economics has grown so rapidly in recent years, it has increased so much in scope and depth, and the new dominance of the empirical approach has so transformed its character, that no one book can do it justice today. To fill this need, the Foundations of Modern Economics Series was conceived. The Series, brief books written by leading specialists, reflects the structure, content, and key scientific and policy issues of each field. Used in combination, the Series provides the material for the basic one-year college course. The analytical core of economics is presented in *Prices and Markets* and *National Income Analysis,* which are basic to the various fields of application. Two books in the Series, *The Evolution of Modern Economics and Economic Development: Past and Present,* can be read without prerequisite and can serve as an introduction to the subject.

The Foundations approach enables an instructor to devise his own course curriculum rather than to follow the format of the traditional textbook. Once analytical principles have been mastered, many sequences of topics can be arranged and specific areas can be explored at length. An instructor not interested in a complete survey course can omit some books and concentrate on a detailed study of a few fields. One-semester courses stressing either macro- or micro-economics can be readily devised. The Instructors Guide to the Series indicates the variety of ways the books in the Series can be used.

The books in the Series are also being used as supplements to the basic textbooks, to permit a fuller curriculum on some topics. Intermediate level courses are using volumes in the Series as the core text and are combining these with various readings.

This Series is an experiment in teaching. The positive response to the first two editions has encouraged us to continue to develop and improve the approach. New books are being added and the previous books revised and undated. The thoughtful reactions of many teachers who have used the books in the past have been of immense help in preparing the third edition.

The books do not offer settled conclusions. They introduce the central problems of each field and indicate how economic analysis enables the reader to think more intelligently about them, to make him a more thoughtful citizen, and to encourage him to pursue the subject further.

Otto Eckstein, *Editor*

Money and Credit:
Impact and Control

Introduction

CHAPTER ONE

Money is one of man's greatest inventions. Try to imagine the operation of a complex industrial society—especially a democratic one—without money. That almost all but the simplest human societies have used money proves that it is an essential tool of civilization. But useful though it may be, money has always been a problem. Inflations and depressions have been among the most serious upheavals of industrial societies—and defects in our monetary arrangements have played an important part in every major inflation and in every major recession we have suffered.

In their efforts to repair the apparent defects in their monetary arrangements, governments have erected elaborate systems to control the issue of currency and the operation of banks. Moreover, the victims of inflations, deflations, devaluations, and financial panics have understood that their troubles were in some way connected with the monetary system, but not exactly how. As a result, monetary disputes become disputes over articles of ideological faith. To most people "sound money" has the same standing as home and mother. But exactly which monetary policy is the "sound" one is not so well-agreed. And on the fringes of the debate there are always a few monetary cranks—the faith-healers of economics—who have found the one monetary system which will solve all the world's problems.

WHY MONEY IS SO USEFUL

Money is one of those things that we take for granted because it is difficult to imagine life without it. And it is so difficult for a complex society to exist without money that the breakdown of one monetary system is immediately followed by the development of a new one.

Money is essentially a device to permit people to exchange goods and services in a more convenient way than by direct barter. A moment's thought will convince you how difficult it would be to conduct an industrial economy by means of direct exchange of goods and services for other goods and services. In a simple agricultural society each family may produce most of what it needs and little of what it does not need. A farmer can exchange small surpluses of food crops, or wood, or wool for the products of specialized artisans such as blacksmiths. The few specialists can re-exchange some of the things they take in trade. But that system works only when most families are almost self-sufficient. In a society where each person spends all his time producing one thing, or a part of one thing, almost everything produced must be sold; and many things are sold several times before they reach the final consumer. We manage to make all these trades because everyone is willing to accept money in exchange for any kind of good or service, in the confident expectation that he can use the money to buy any other kind of good or service. You can get an idea of the role money plays in our economy by noting how much it is used. The total volume of money transactions in 1970 was 10 *trillion.* About 60 per cent of the transactions were financial payments associated with trading in securities or other assets. The remaining 40 per cent—$4 *trillion* worth—were payments associated with the production, distribution, and consumption of goods and services.

WHY MONEY CAUSES SO MUCH TROUBLE

By using money we can divide the exchange process into two parts. It is a great deal easier to exchange goods and services for money, and then exchange the money for other goods and services, than to exchange one set of goods and services directly for another. But the fact that money enables us to break the exchange process into two parts is the source of a great deal of trouble. If goods can be obtained for money, it always looks easy to get something for nothing—or for very little—by manufacturing money. For thousands of years monetary systems using metal coins were upset by counterfeiters, coin-clippers, or governments trying to finance themselves by minting short-weight coins. With the development of paper money, the profitability of the private manufacture of bank notes and the efforts of governments to finance wars by the use of the printing press have produced numerous inflations, devaluations, and financial panics.

Breaking the exchange process into two parts causes another set of difficulties. In a barter world no one can sell goods or services without buying at the same time. But when we use money it is possible to "sell now, buy later," meanwhile holding money. Ordinarily, this can be done without causing harm: some people are increasing their holdings of money by selling more than they buy, while others are doing the opposite. But when many people try to accumulate money at once, by selling the fruits of production without buying anything, there is trouble. Some people will find themselves unemployed or unable to sell what they have produced.

When people try to accumulate money by spending less than they receive, they do not add to the total stock of money. But they do slow down the rate at which it changes hands. And when people try to reduce their holdings of money by spending more than they have received, the money doesn't disappear—it just moves faster. Unlike most things, money isn't used up when it's used.

When the amount of money in existence is increased *or* when the rate at which money moves increases, there is more monetary demand for goods and services. Within limits that's fine. Indeed, in an economy with a growing labor force and increasing productivity, we want the demand for goods and services to increase from one year to the next. But you can have too much of a good thing. If the demand for goods and services increases very rapidly, the output of goods and services can't keep up and prices will have to rise.

On the other hand, if the amount of money decreases *or* if its rate of movement slows down, then prices, output, and employment will decline.

Every major depression has been accompanied by a substantial decline in the money supply, and often by a complete collapse of the banking system. Among the many causes responsible for our major depressions, money and banking difficulties have always been prominent.

People have been using money for thousands of years and they've always had trouble with it. Sometimes people are complaining about inflation and blaming it on an excessive increase in the money supply. Sometimes the trouble is recession—unemployment, idle factories, and falling prices. Then they complain that the money supply is being kept too small. There is seldom just the right amount of money circulating. A variety of devices for properly controlling the money supply have been tried in the last few hundred years. The next two chapters trace the development of monetary arrangements from the period of exclusive reliance on metal coin, through the era of privately issued paper money, down to the present system of control by the Federal Reserve System.

CONTROL OF MONEY AS AN INSTRUMENT OF ECONOMIC POLICY

It is easy enough to see that money is important to all of us and to see why, after centuries of experiments, we have made elaborate arrangements to control its supply in the public interest. But this only raises new questions how that power is to be used.

The money supply influences expenditures for goods and services. Properly managed, it can promote four of the major objectives of economic policy: full employment, price stability, growth, and balance-of-payments equilibrium.

The Federal Reserve System has the job of managing the money supply. By changing the money supply it influences the behavior of banks and other lenders. The resulting changes in interest rates and in the availability of credit will influence business investment, construction of houses, and other types of spending, and hence the performance of the entire economy. This is the central topic of this book.

Chapters 3 and 4 discuss the impact of Federal Reserve policy on the behavior of commercial banks. Chapter 5 examines the behavior of other lenders and borrowers in the capital markets. Chapter 6 shows how interest rates are determined, and how monetary policy can be used to control expenditure and employment. Chapter 7 reviews the practical effects of Federal Reserve policy. Finally, in Chapter 8, we consider some of the conflicts of objectives which make monetary policy a continuing subject of controversy.

The Nature and Evolution of Money

CHAPTER TWO

Direct barter is so unwieldy that anthropologists have found some form of money in use in most "primitive" societies. An immense variety of things have been used for money at one time or another—shells, tobacco, feathers, even sharks' teeth. Gold, silver, and copper were used most widely, even long before the invention of coinage. The first coins are supposed to have been struck around 700 B.C., but gold and silver were in use by the Babylonians as early as 2000 B.C.

When we say that Yap islanders use stones for money, we must have some test or definition in mind by which to tell whether something is or is not being used for money. Money is anything that is generally acceptable in exchange for goods and services and for payment of debts. It need not have any other use. People mainly accept it in the expectation of passing it on to someone else in a further exchange. An essential characteristic of money is general confidence in its acceptability as a medium of exchange.

WHAT CAN SERVE AS MONEY?

Until recently, most of the things used as money had a certain intrinsic value. They had some use for purposes other than money. Frequently they were valued for personal ornamentation before they were used as money. In addition, they generally had certain other properties which made them convenient to use as money. They were durable—i.e., did not deteriorate with time or wear out quickly when handled. They had a relatively high value per unit of weight so that they could be carried easily and were divisible into fairly small units. Gold, silver, and copper possessed all these properties to a greater degree than most other commodities, which is probably why they were used as money in so many places for so long.

The historical origin of a particular thing such as money may lie in its intrinsic usefulness. But once it is established in use as money, its acceptability comes to depend simply on everyone's belief that everyone else will accept it. Long before the advent of paper money, there were many cases of societies with money which no one wanted for anything except to use in exchanges. The stones of the Yap islanders serve no ornamental or any other purpose. Some of them are too large to move, but everyone knows who owns them. Indeed, one of them retained its value and was still used after it had fallen off a cliff into the sea.

There are all sorts of examples of useless monies. The acceptability of money does not rest on its usefulness, but rather on confidence in its continued acceptability. Money is as money does.

Many people think that the dollar is valuable because of its now somewhat tenuous connection with gold. But ask yourself what would happen to the value of gold if the U.S. Treasury refused to give $35 for every ounce of gold offered to it. Does gold impart value to paper dollars—or do the dollars impart value to gold?

KINDS OF MONEY IN THE U.S.

There are three major types of money used in the United States today—coins, paper money, and checking deposits.

Until about 300 years ago metal coins were the only kind of money in use. But in the United States, and almost everywhere else today, coins are only small change. In the U.S. in 1970 there were $6 billion worth of coins in use, compared with $52 billion worth of paper money in circulation and bank checking accounts amounting to $163 billion.

The value of the metal in our coins is deliberately kept below the nominal value of the coins so that it won't be profitable to melt them down for their metallic content. When the price of silver threatened to reach the point where it would pay people to melt down dimes and quarters, the Treasury quickly substituted copper and nickel. The U.S. mint stands ready to supply coins in exchange for other kinds of money, and it will reverse the exchange whenever banks bring in surpluses of coin. The amount of coin in circulation, then, is just what the public wants it to be.

Most of our paper money consists of Federal Reserve Notes issued by the 12 Federal Reserve Banks. A small amount of the paper money in circulation consists of "fossils"—paper money issued for one reason or another in the past. These include U.S. Notes (the Civil War "greenbacks"), Treasury Notes of 1890, National Bank Notes, and Federal Reserve Bank Notes (as distinguished from Federal Reserve Notes). The long-familiar one-dollar silver certificates have been replaced by Federal Reserve Notes.

The largest element in our money supply consists of deposits—i.e., checking accounts in commercial banks. Checking accounts are nothing more than bookkeeping entries in the records of banks; they are not embodied in physical form like coins and bills. But they are money as much as the coins in our pockets, because checking accounts function as money. They are generally acceptable in exchange for goods and services and for payment of debts. Indeed, the volume of payments made by check is far greater than the amount of payments made with currency and coin.

Table 2-1 (A) MONEY SUPPLY IN THE UNITED STATES OCTOBER 31, 1970 (Millions of Dollars)

Silver dollars	$ 485
Other coin	5,997
Other	622
Total Treasury currency and coin	7,104
Federal Reserve Notes	51,652
Total currency and coin	58,756
Less currency and coin in banks	3,571
Currency and coin held by the public	55,185
Demand deposits (checking accounts)	163,300
Total money supply	$218,485

Table 2-1 (B) SUPPLY OF NEAR MONEY IN THE UNITED STATES OCTOBER 31, 1970 (Millions of Dollars)

Time and savings deposits in commercial banks	$221,800
Deposits at mutual savings banks	70,200
Savings-and-loan shares	142,697
U.S. Savings Bonds	52,200
U.S. securities due in less than 1 year	111,636
Total	$598,533

Source: Federal Reserve Bulletin, December, 1970. Data not seasonally adjusted.

We are all familiar with bank deposits and with the use of checks. But what is a bank deposit? It is not, as we are inclined to think, a pile of coins and bills in the vaults of a bank. A bank deposit is a promise on the part of the bank to pay immediately on request (on demand) of the customer who owns the deposit. It is a liability of the bank. The bank owes the owner of a bank deposit and will pay him or another party he designates in coins, paper money, or with a check on another bank if he wishes. A check is an order to the bank to pay a specific sum.

Of course, banks do have coins and bills in their vaults, but the amount they hold is only about 2 per cent of the deposit liabilities of banks. The vault cash held by a bank is an asset of the bank along with its other assets—government bonds, mortgages, and the IOU's of business firms to whom it has extended loans.

NEAR MONIES

We consider demand deposits to be money because they can be used to pay for goods and services by means of checks. Commercial banks have other deposit liabilities called time deposits or savings deposits which differ from demand deposits only in the fact that they cannot be transferred by check. If you have a savings account and want to buy something, you have to present your pass book at your bank, withdraw currency, and then pay cash for what you buy. You cannot pay for anything with a savings deposit.

The same thing holds true for deposits in savings banks and savings-and-loan shares. Nonetheless, time and savings deposits in commercial banks, deposits in mutual savings banks, and savings-and-loan shares are regarded by their holders as almost the same thing as money, because they can be quickly and cheaply changed for money. The claims just mentioned, along with some others such as short-term U.S. Treasury securities and U.S. Savings Bonds, are frequently called "near monies" or "money substitutes."

THE EVOLUTION OF MONEY

Through regulation of commercial banks, the Federal Reserve System indirectly controls the amount of demand deposits. Thus the amount of money in existence is controlled by a public agency. It was not always this way. Our present monetary system reflects 300 years of experience with a variety of arrangements. You will get a clearer understanding of our present system if you think of it as the product of a gradual evolution based on that (frequently unhappy) experience. In the remainder of this chapter we will review the major steps in that evolutionary process.

The Unreliability of Metallic Money

Faced with the problems of inflation and deflation and with constant controversy over monetary policy, some people are inclined to demand a return to the "good old days" of a monetary system based on gold coin. But the "golden age of gold coin," like other golden ages, is mythical. The opportunity to get something for nothing by alloying supposedly pure gold and silver coins with cheaper metals appears to have been irresistible. The story of coinage in the ancient world is quickly revealed by Table 2-2, which shows changes in the Roman coinage.

Table 2-2 **THE SILVER CONTENT OF ROME'S CURRENCY**

Reign Began (A.D.)	*Emperor*	*Per Cent Silver*
98	Trajan	93
117	Hadrian	87
138	Antoninus Pius	75
161	Marcus Aurelius	68
193	Septimius Severus	50
218	Elagabalus	43
235	Maximinus	35
238	Gordian	28
244	Philip	0.5
268	Claudius Victorinus	0.02

Source: Business Review, Federal Reserve Bank of Philadelphia, January, 1960.

In western European monarchies, the story was much the same. Henry VIII was known as "old coppernose," because the silver on his coins wore off quickly, revealing the copper below. And while governments systematically debased the coinage, free enterprise did its bit. People clipped coins or shook them up in bags to collect the abraded gold scrapings.

When monarchs made two coins out of one by mixing precious metals with base metals, they did it to finance their expenditures—to fight wars, keep up lavish courts, or build monuments. Currency debasement led to rising prices, not because the coins contained less gold but because more of them were struck and they were spent for goods and services. Prices had to rise because expenditures rose faster than the potential output of the economy.

Coinage debasement wasn't the only cause of inflation. There was widespread inflation in Europe during the sixteenth century after the discovery of gold and silver mines in the Spanish possessions in America. Again prices went up because more coins were struck and they were spent rapidly.

Metallic coinages were seldom satisfactory, because the supply of money depended on the whims of monarchs and chance discoveries of mines. Coinage problems became unimportant only when paper money and bank deposits became the common form of money.

The Development of Bank-Note Money

When the Roman Empire collapsed, the highly developed monetary systems of the ancient world collapsed with it. Subsistence agriculture and petty barter dominated the scene. Money was used only in the trickle of long-distance trade in luxuries which survived.

As trade revived, money became important again, and the character of the new monetary system was strongly influenced by the conditions of trade. Because transport was expensive and uncertain, wide price differences existed between areas producing different products. Long-distance trade was profitable, but anyone who carried a large sum of coin on a long journey ran a considerable risk of losing it to robbers or pirates. Even in towns there was considerable danger of robbery.

The rising volume of economic activity made many people eager to borrow and willing to pay high rates of interest. Merchants wanted to borrow to buy goods to sell abroad. Nobles rich in land but poor in money borrowed against their rents once feudal services were commuted into money rents. Monarchs were eager to borrow to finance their wars.

These conditions provided the basis for the development of modern money and banking systems. To avoid carrying money long distances, merchants worked out arrangements for canceling debts. At the medieval fairs, merchants worked out clearing arrangements. Merchants from different places had sold goods at the fair and bought others. Instead of settling each transaction in coin, each merchant paid into a common pool the excess of the amount he bought over the amount he sold, or received from it the excess of his sales over his purchases. This arrangement reduced the amount of coin that had to be carried to and from the fair.

The same technique was then applied at a distance. An Italian merchant, shipping goods to England, would sell his claim for payment against the English buyer to another Italian merchant who had arranged to buy in England. The Italian buying in England was then able to pay his supplier by sending him the IOU of another Englishman. The English buyer would then pay the English seller. Coin moved from one Englishman to another and from one Italian to another, but no coin had to be moved between the countries. The claims involved were represented by bills of exchange—orders by the seller to the buyer to pay the bearer the amount due. These were something like bank checks except that they were drawn by one private individual on another. After a time, bills of exchange drawn on well-known and reliable merchants were passed from hand to hand to make several different payments. This was very similar to the case in which a check on a bank is passed from hand to hand and acquires several endorsements before it is presented to the bank.

A number of people began to act as intermediaries in the financing of loans, accepting coin from individuals with surpluses, and lending to others The people involved in this business have varied backgrounds. Some were merchants who got into the business of borrowing and relending as a sideline; some began buying and selling bills of exchange; some were lawyers who arranged the legal details of loan transactions; some were goldsmiths who became connected with finance by arranging gold shipments and weighing, assaying, and storing coin.

As early as the thirteenth century, Italian banks had begun accepting coin and agreeing to repay it on demand. They lent out most of these deposits, relying on new deposits to offset the withdrawal of old ones. They kept on hand only a relatively small reserve of coins to guard against withdrawals temporarily exceeding new deposits. They paid interest on their deposit accounts and their customers fully understood that the bank had lent out most of the coin it received.

For a long time legal problems prevented the use of checks, but Italian banks were prepared to transfer ownership of deposits from one person to another through bookkeeping entries. But both parties to the transaction had to appear in person.

In England, goldsmiths became predominant in the banking business, and it was the English goldsmiths who led the way in the development of bank-note currency. The English goldsmiths accepted deposits—with a promise to pay on demand—and then lent most of what they received. They gave interest-bearing receipts and permitted the holders to transfer ownership of deposits by endorsing these receipts. Presently, to make endorsements unnecessary, the receipts were made payable to the bearer. Then, because it was so convenient to make payments by giving goldsmiths' receipts, customers became willing to take non-interest-bearing receipts. As a final step, the receipts were issued in round numbers and engraved on standard forms. These were bank notes, the earliest form of paper money.

The use of bank notes developed rapidly. As soon as the acceptability of bank-note currency was established, note-issuing banks sprang up all over England. Many of these banks did no deposit business at all. The organizers of the bank put up a certain amount of capital in coin. They then printed notes—promises to pay coin on demand. They lent the notes to business firms and made a profit by charging interest. Thus the balance sheet of a note-issuing bank at the time of organization would look like this:

Assets		*Liabilities*	
Loans	$50,000	Notes outstanding	$50,000
Coin	$10,000	Capital	$10,000

In effect, the bank had exchanged its promises to pay for those of the business firms to whom it lent. It was able to collect interest on this exchange because it was prepared to meet its promises to pay on demnad. The banker "created" money but he did not create wealth.

The fact that debts circulate as money and that banks do create money seems at least as odd as the use of sharks' teeth for money among primitive peoples. But the development of bank-note currency was the culmination of several hundred years of experience with the use of various kinds of evidences of debt to avoid the risks and inconveniences of carrying and storing coin. It was also a response to the generally poor state of the coinage and the willingness of business and government to pay high enough interest rates to make banking a worthwhile occupation.

Reserves and Bank Crises

Every note-issuing bank was faced with the problem of determining how many notes it could safely issue in relation to the coin contributed by the partners. A bank could increase its interest income by expanding its loans and note issues. Obviously, every bank wanted to keep as high a ratio of notes outstanding to coin reserves (i.e., as low a ratio of reserves to notes) as possible. At the same time, it had to maintain large enough reserves to meet all requests to pay out coin in exchange for its notes. In ordinary circumstances a relatively small reserve sufficed. Notes would be returned to a bank by customers wanting coin to make wage or other payments (notes were issued only in large denominations), or they might be returned by other banks which had paid out coin for them and now sought reimbursement. But the bank would also receive payment for some of its loans in gold or notes of other banks which could be exchanged for gold. Ordinarily, these inflows and outflows would roughly cancel. A coin reserve was needed only to balance off the difference between daily inflows and outflows. For that purpose a reserve of only a small percentage of outstanding notes would suffice.

But should there be any doubts about a bank's ability to meet claims against it, even a very large reserve in relation to notes outstanding might not suffice. A rumor that a bank had lent to merchants involved in an unsuccessful speculation or a hint of any kind of mismanagement could start a run on a bank. Other banks and merchants would hurry to present the bank's notes for payment in coin before it was too late. Their action would frighten others and the bank's holdings of coin would quickly be used up. A solvent bank might be able to borrow from others to meet the crisis, but whether it could get enough help quickly enough was always a question. A banker's life was anything but peaceful.

A bank which was unable to meet a run had to "stop payments"—i.e., announce its inability to give coin for its notes. The note-holders did not necessarily lose because of this action. The bank might ultimately collect all its loans and pay off its notes. But meanwhile its failure might involve others. Holders of the bank's notes were unable to use them to pay their debts and sometimes went bankrupt. Runs might start on other banks whose customers had gone bankrupt, or merely because the failure of one bank raised fears about the status of the others. Throughout the nineteenth century English and American commercial life was upset every few years by commercial crises marked by bank and business failures.

Inconvertible Paper Money

In spite of these difficulties, bank notes, which were promises to pay gold coin on demand, came to be generally accepted in exchange for goods and services, and for payment of debts. *In other words, they became money.*

Originally, bank notes were simply promises to pay money—no different from any other IOU's. Most promises to pay are not generally acceptable in exchange for foods and services because (1) they do not promise immediate payment; (2) the ability and willingness of the issuer (debtor) to make payment is subject to question; (3) legal formalities are necessary to transfer ownership.

Early bankers were able to establish the general acceptability of their notes by (1) achieving almost unquestioned credit standing by meeting their obligations without fail over a long period; and (2) creating a form of IOU which was payable on demand, readily identifiable, and transferable without legal formalities.

At first, bank notes were regarded as claims which served as useful substitutes for money, but only gold and silver coin was regarded as real money. With the passage of time, however, people ceased to draw any distinction between the real thing and the substitute. Bank notes were just as readily acceptable in trading transactions as gold coin, so they were just as much money as was gold coin. Nonetheless, bank notes still had to meet the test of redemption for gold coin. People who needed coin to make payments in foreign countries or for some other special purpose or who simply distrusted banks had the right to ask the banker for gold coin in exchange for his notes. If the banker failed to deliver, everyone else presented his notes and the bank had to close. But though bank money had to meet the redemption test, it was clearly money because it was generally acceptable as a medium of exchange.

The final step in this evolution was reached when people became so used to bank notes that they were prepared to accept notes which could not be converted into gold. The notes of the Bank of England and the Federal Reserve are formal liabilities of a bank—promises to pay something. But neither institution will in fact convert its notes into anything else. People became willing to accept bank notes after convertibility into gold ceased because everyone was confident that everyone else would accept them. Once sufficient confidence in their acceptability had been built up over the years, the convertibility prop to confidence could be removed like a temporary scaffolding.

DEPOSIT BANKING

Use of bank notes in England was established by the end of the seventeenth century. Deposit banking and the use of checks to transfer ownership of deposits developed more slowly. Early bank checks were simply informal notes from a depositor to his banker instructing the bank to pay a certain amount to the person named in the check. By the end of the eighteenth century the use of checks was common, particularly among London merchants and financial houses.[1] As the volume of trade grew with the progress of the commercial and industrial revolutions, merchants found it increasingly convenient to use checks instead of bank notes. The large merchants in London began to bring gold coin and bank notes into the London deposit banks and to pay by check.

At first glance, a demand deposit may not seem to be much like a bank note, but in two fundamental respects they are the same: (1) demand deposits, like bank notes, are liabilities of banks (promises to pay standard money on demand); (2) both are used as a means of payment for goods and services.

The difference lies in the way in which they circulate. Bank notes circulate from hand to hand and can be used many times without ever appearing at a bank. On the other hand, demand deposits circulate by check and most of the checks drawn on the deposits of one bank will be deposited at another. The receiving bank then has a claim on the bank on which the check was drawn. Every day every bank receives checks on other banks and it is necessary for banks to settle their claims on one another. The method of settlement is called clearing checks.

Suppose there are two banks in the community; each bank will receive checks on the other each day. On a particular day bank *A* may receive in deposits $10,000 worth of checks drawn on *B* while *B* receives $12,000 worth of checks on *A*. Representatives of the two banks meet each day and exchange the checks received. *A* owes *B* $2,000 which must be paid in notes or coin. Notice that only $2,000 of notes and coin have to move in order to carry out $22,000 worth of transactions.

We have pointed out the similarities between bank notes and demand deposits—both are demand claims against a bank and both can "circulate" as means of payment. There is another similarity. Demand deposits, like bank notes, are *fractional reserve money*. If you looked at the books of one of the London deposit banks, you would find that they did not appear very different

[1] The Bank of England was granted a monopoly of note issue in the London area, leading to organization of a number of banks which accepted deposits subject to check but did not issue notes.

from those of a note-issuing bank. The statement might look something like this:

Assets		Liabilities	
Loans	$80,000	Demand deposits	$100,000
Currency and coin	$30,000	Capital	$ 10,000

The bank has deposits of several times its "reserve" of currency and coin, just as a note-issuing bank has notes outstanding of a value which is several times as great as its reserve. In fact, banks create deposits just as they manufacture bank notes.

HOW BANKS CREATE MONEY

The balance sheet of a deposit bank resembles that of a note-issuing bank. But there is an important difference in the way in which banks create deposits. A note-issuing bank started with a certain amount of capital and lent an amount of notes representing several times as much. A deposit bank begins in a different way. It obtains some initial funds from customers who bring in currency and coin and take a deposit credit on the bank's books (against which checks can be written) in exchange.

Deposit banking is based on the principle that all the customers who have brought funds to the bank will not withdraw them at once. On any day some of the customers will withdraw funds in cash or by checks presented by other banks at the clearinghouse. But other customers will increase their deposits by bringing in cash or checks on other banks.

Experience shows that in normal circumstances deposits and withdrawals tend to balance. A bank needs a cash reserve because deposits and withdrawals do not balance exactly. Banks have generally found that reserves of less than 20 per cent of deposits are adequate to meet occasional excesses of withdrawals over deposits.

Deposit Expansion Stage 1

A bank, having received some cash from customers who have brought funds to the bank, is therefore in a position to make loans or investments. A bank, say bank *A,* starting out with deposits in currency and coin of $100,000, might feel safe to lend $80,000. In a check-using community, the bank would make its loans by giving the borrowers the right to draw checks against it. The right to draw checks is called a demand deposit even though the borrower hasn't deposited anything. (If you like, you may consider that the bank gives currency to the borrower when it makes the loan and that he then deposits it in the bank.) These transactions are summarized below:

1. Customers deposit coin and bank notes in exchange for the right to draw checks. These changes would appear in the bank's balance sheet:

Bank A

Assets	*Liabilities*
Notes and Coins + $100,000	Customers' Deposits + $100,000

2. The bank needs a reserve of notes and coin equal only to 20 per cent of deposit claims. It lends an amount equal to its "excess" reserve. It makes the loan by giving the borrowers deposit credit and receiving their promissory notes in exchange. These changes would appear in the bank's balance sheet:

Bank A

Assets	*Liabilities*
Promissory Notes + 80,000	Borrowers' Deposits + 80,000

3. Add the changes in steps 1 and 2:

Bank A

Assets		*Liabilities*	
Notes and Coin	+ 100,000	Customers' Deposits	+ 100,000
Promissory Notes	+ 80,000	Borrowers' Deposits	+ 80,000
	180,000		180,000

Of course, the borrowers will spend the proceeds of the loans very quickly. Otherwise they would not have borrowed. They will write checks or withdraw currency. Then the bank will lose a corresponding amount of its reserve in currency and coin. Therefore, the bank can afford to lend only *an amount equal to the excess of currency and coin over the amount it requires as reserves.*

Our deposit bank has manufactured money. After the bank has made its loans, there is $80,000 more of money in existence than there was before. The deposit claims of the original depositors are money, since the holders expect to use them to buy things. And the borrowers also have money either in currency or in the deposit claims they were given when they borrowed. When they spend it, the money doesn't disappear—someone else receives it. So although the mechanics are somewhat different, banks which accept demand deposits subject to check, manufacture money just as note-issuing banks do. The acceptability of the deposit claims against banks, of course, requires confidence in banks, just as in the case of bank notes. Once bank notes paved the way, it was easier for people to get used to exchanging bank deposits through use of checks.

MULTIPLE EXPANSION OF DEPOSITS

We mentioned that borrowers will quickly draw on the deposits they received as loans. If they took cash and the cash remained in circulation, that would be the end of the story. But suppose the borrowers drew checks against their accounts and the recipients deposited the checks in another bank, *B*. The bank receiving the checks would present them at the clearinghouse and (leaving other transactions aside) would collect currency and coin from the first bank. A summary of these transactions follows:

4. The borrowers draw checks on bank *A* which are received by customers of bank *B*. Bank *A* pays the other bank in notes and coin. Changes in the banks' balance sheets are shown below:

Bank A

Liabilities	*Assets*
Notes and Coin − 80,000	Deposits − 80,000

Bank B

Assets	*Liabilities*
Notes and Coin + 80,000	Deposits + 80,000

5. Adding the changes in (4) to those in (3), the net changes in bank *A*'s balance sheet now look like this:

Bank A

Assets		*Liabilities*	
Notes and Coins	+ 20,000	Deposits	+ 100,000
Promissory Notes	+ 80,000		

Notice that bank *A* has a reserve equal to 20 per cent of its deposits. Its balance sheet looks very much like that of a note-issuing bank. But as we have seen, it arrived at that position by an entirely different route. It didn't create an amount of money equal to five times its initial deposit. It created an amount of money equal to four-fifths of its initial deposit. Then all the new deposits were withdrawn and it lost four-fifths of the reserves obtained from the initial deposit. It was then left with a reserve equal to one-fifth of the initial deposit. By lending out its excess reserves, bank *A* ends up with reserves just equal to the desired 20 per cent of its deposits.

Deposit Expansion Stage 2

Bank *B* would have no reason to distinguish its deposits of $80,000 from any other and would therefore have more reserves than it needed. Having acquired $80,000 in coin against new deposits of the same amount, it needs a reserve of $16,000 and has excess reserves of $64,000. It is therefore in a position to make loans of $64,000. The borrowers will be given deposit credit for $64,000 but may be expected to withdraw it in cash or by check very shortly. When they have done so, bank *B* will be left with $16,000 in coin and deposit liabilities of $80,000—a 20 per cent ratio of reserves to deposits. Bank *B* has now created another $64,000, since the depositors of the $80,000 regard their claims as money and someone else has $64,000 in coin. The two banks together have therefore created $144,000. (Total deposits have increased by $180,000, and $64,000 is circulating as coins, making a total of $244,000 from the original deposit of $100,000.) The transactions just described are summarized below:

6. Bank *B* is in the same position as bank *A* after step 1. It needs a reserve of only 20 per cent against the $80,000 of deposits received from checks on *A*. It needs a reserve of $16,000 and has excess reserves of $64,000. To increase earnings, it lends that amount.

Bank B

Assets		*Liabilities*	
Loans	+ 64,000	Deposits	+ 64,000

The borrowers will write checks on *B* which will be deposited in another bank, *C*. *B* pays *C* with notes and coin.

Bank B

Assets		*Liabilities*	
Notes and Coins	— 64,000	Deposits	— 64,000

Bank C

Assets		*Liabilities*	
Notes and Coins	+ 64,000	Deposits	+ 64,000

As in the case of bank *A*, the withdrawals from deposits created by bank *B*'s loans might be withdrawn in cash or by check. Suppose they are all withdrawn by check and the checks are deposited in a third bank, *C*. Then the whole process could be repeated with bank *C* "creating" another chunk of money 80 per cent as large as its predecessor. Obviously, the process could go on indefinitely, with the amount of money created at each step getting smaller and smaller.

Ultimately, the whole set of banks would create an amount of money (in the form of deposits) equal to several times the amount of the original deposit. How much would depend on the size of the reserve in coin they felt it necessary to hold, and on the proportion of the proceeds of their loans taken in cash instead of in checks to be deposited in other banks.

PUBLIC CONTROL OF THE MONEY SUPPLY

The issue of bank notes was eventually taken over by government controlled institutions and the notes ceased to be convertible into gold coin. But the "issue" of bank deposits remained in private hands. And even today a private bank must be prepared to convert deposits into other forms of money such as currency or coins on demand.

At the end of the eighteenth century it was widely believed that the money supply, like everything else, would be automatically regulated by private competition, provided the government kept its hands off. But, as we have already pointed out, individual banks frequently did get into trouble leading to economy-wide disturbances throughout the nineteenth century. The total money supply moved erratically, sometimes increasing rapidly, sometimes declining abruptly. The record of private competition in regulating the money supply was unsatisfactory. In England the Bank of England was given the power and the responsibility of controlling the money supply and thus solved many, though by no means all, of the problems of a privately controlled money supply. American monetary history followed a different path, although ultimately a central bank was also created to control the money supply.

SUMMARY

Many different things have been used as money at one time or another. Some of them have been useful objects but others were merely tokens. Anything can serve as money so long as everyone is confident of its acceptability in exchange for goods and services. It does not matter whether that confidence originates in law, custom, or in the intrinsic value of the objects.

Our money consists mainly of demand deposits—checking accounts—and Federal Reserve notes, and of relatively small amounts of coin and other kinds of paper money.

Our present monetary system is the result of hundreds of years of evolution in the use of money. Merchants exchanged promises to pay in order to avoid the use of coin. The use of bank notes gradually developed out of that experience. Later another kind of claim against banks—the demand deposit—came into widespread use.

Nowadays bank notes are issued only by government-sponsored institutions like the Federal Reserve Bank and the Bank of England. But demand deposits are still created by private banks.

Note-issuing banks were able to issue an amount of notes equal to several times the amount of their reserves in coin. They were able to do so because only a fraction of those receiving the bank notes wanted to redeem them in coin.

Deposit banks also have deposit liabilities equal to several times the amount of their reserves. But the process by which banks "create" deposits equal to several times the amount of their reserves is more complicated than the note-issue process, involving the withdrawal of deposits created by loans, their redeposit in another bank, and further loans on the basis of the new deposits.

The Development of Money and Banking in the United States

CHAPTER THREE

Before the Revolution, the American colonies got along with a rather makeshift monetary system. English and foreign coins circulated simultaneously. The colonies frequently issued paper money as a means of covering their expenses without resort to taxation—even with representation. The amounts they issued grew until the paper money depreciated in terms of gold and silver coin and in terms of goods. The English government finally prohibited the colonial governments from issuing paper money.

During the Revolution the Continental Congress issued large amounts of paper dollars to pay for the war, such large amounts relative to the resources of the country that these "continentals" eventually became a synonym for worthlessness. They were eventually redeemed at $.01 on the dollar. After the adoption of the Constitution, the federal government began to mint gold and silver coins. Except for temporary issues in the War of 1812 and the Mexican War, the Treasury issued no paper money until the Civil War.

Although the federal government refrained from issuing paper money, banks entered the field enthusiastically. Every state chartered banks, often with very little regulation. Checks still were not widely used. Banks made their profits by lending their own notes, which were then put into circulation by the borrowers. The reserve for redemption of the notes in coin was provided by the capital subscribed by the proprietors. The bank which could keep the largest number of notes in circulation per dollar of reserve earned the highest return on capital. Many banks maintained adequate reserves and were able to redeem all the notes returned for coin. But others, particularly in some of the western and southern states, issued notes with little concern for the problem of redemption.

In 1861 a writer in the *Chicago Tribune* said the "bank nuisance has become unbearable." According to that writer many banks made it their chief business to manufacture and put out as many notes as they could by any contrivance keep in circulation, regardless of the dearth of reserves. Some were "merely banks of circulation without capital and doing no business at their nominal locations," the notes being issued at goodly distances from the place of redemption so as to delay presentation. Many main offices where redemptions were made "were located in the depths of forests where there were few human inhabitations, but plenty of wildcats. Thus they came to be known as the wildcat banks." Most of the Chicago banks issued notes through agent banks in Georgia. In addition to the factor of risk, bank notes sank in value in proportion to distance and other difficulties in presenting them for redemption.

From the Revolution until the Civil War the commercial life of the U.S. was constantly plagued with the problems posed by the circulation of counterfeit bank notes, or bank notes issued by closed or non-existent banks.

This situation persisted because among farmers and others in the expanding west there was an intense demand for credit. They wanted to invest in land, buildings, and equipment and resisted attempts to regulate banking because they feared that their access to credit would be limited.

In the pre-Civil War period, two abortive attempts to provide some central control of banking was made. The First Bank of the United States operated from 1797 to 1810 and the Second Bank of the United States from 1816 to 1836. These banks were chartered by the federal government and had a much larger initial capital than other banks. They were depositories for federal government funds. Though they were private banks, they attempted to exercise some control over private bank-note issues by promptly returning for redemption in gold all the notes of other banks which they received. In that way a bank which issued too large an amount of notes in relation to its reserves of coin was soon drained of reserves and failed.

This check to the expansion of bank credit was resented in the expanding western sections of the country, and neither Bank lasted long because Congress refused to renew their charters. From 1836 until the Civil War there were constant demands to do something about the uncertain state of the currency, but Congress took no action until it was forced by the Civil War.

During the Civil War the federal government printed paper money—"greenbacks"—to finance the war. In addition, the government established the national banking system; it authorized the chartering of national banks which were given the privilege of issuing notes secured by U.S. bonds. These notes were declared "legal tender," which means that anyone who offers to pay his debts with them has discharged his obligation. At the same time, a tax was levied on notes issued by state-chartered banks, which made them unprofitable. Most of the state-chartered banks took out new charters as national banks. For the first time, the U.S. had a banking system which was subject to a uniform set of regulations and a currency which was directly regulated by the federal government.

Growth of Deposit Banking

But just when the currency problem seemed to be solved, the importance of note issues in the total money supply began to decline. The rapid industrialization after the Civil War led to a rapid increase in the volume of payments to be made. Bank notes serve well enough for small-scale payments between individuals in direct contact, but payment by check is obviously much more convenient for business firms engaged in large-scale transactions. Within a few years after the Civil War a large number of state-chartered banks which specialized in deposit banking were organized.

DEFECTS OF THE NATIONAL BANKING SYSTEM

The national banking system was a great improvement over the pre-Civil War system but was very inadequate for a country which was coming of age as a great industrial nation. The period between the Civil War and the First World War was one of great industrial expansion. But this spectacular growth was periodically interrupted by financial panics and depression. In 1878, 1883, and 1907 there were waves of bank failures, stock prices collapsed, thousands of business firms failed. These panics were followed by depressions marked by low industrial production and high unemployment. Many factors helped to produce these episodes of panic and depression, but everyone agreed that the weaknesses of the banking system were partly responsible and certainly intensified depressions after they began.

The national banking system effectively prevented the overissue of notes by wildcat banks, but it went too far in the other direction. An expanding country needs an increasing amount of currency for hand-to-hand transactions, and it needs more at some seasons of the year than at others. The national banking system provided a uniform currency but made no provision for varying the amount with the needs of the country. Every fall, businesses would withdraw currency from banks to pay farmers for crops. Banks would have to pay out their reserves. There were thousands of banks, many of them very small and many badly managed. Some banks found themselves without enough reserves to meet currency withdrawals and had to close.

The problem was compounded by the fact that small-town banks were allowed to keep part of their reserves on deposit with large city banks. When country banks needed currency, they drew on those deposits. The city banks then had to find the necessary currency quickly. In most years the banking system managed to stagger through the fall season with only a modest number of bank failures. But periodically some event—a decline in stock prices, the failure of an important business firm, or a gold outflow to pay for imports—would raise fears about the solvency of banks. People would then try to convert deposits into currency and that demand, on top of the seasonal demand, would be too much for the banking system. Some important bank would fail and that would intensify the public's fears. Every bank would be subject to heavy withdrawals of currency. They would all try to raise cash by selling securities and calling loans, thus depressing security prices and causing business failures. Clearly, what was needed was some device which would keep the volume of currency and deposits under control—avoid the excesses of free banking—yet permit sufficient flexibility to meet the needs of a changing economy.

After the panic of 1907, demand for changes in the banking system became intense and a National Monetary Commission was established. It delivered a voluminous report in 1911 covering the experience of the American banking systems and of foreign systems. The recommendations of the report, though considerably revised, became the basis for the establishment of the Federal Reserve System in 1914.

THE FEDERAL RESERVE SYSTEM

The National Monetary Commission recommended the establishment of a central bank modeled on long-established European institutions like the Bank of England and the Bank of France. In deference to the forces of regionalism and agrarian fear of control by eastern financial centers, the Federal Reserve Act established not 1 but 12 banks. The country was divided into 12 Federal Reserve Districts each served by a Federal Reserve Bank. The banks are nominally private corporations whose stock is owned by the commercial banks they serve. In practice, the broad policy of the whole system is controlled by the Board of Governors of the Federal Reserve System, who are appointed by the President. Many decisions are left to the officers and directors of the 12 banks, so that the system provides a uniform basic monetary policy whose detailed administration can be responsive to the special needs and conditions of the different parts of the country.

All national banks were required to become members of the Federal Reserve System; state-chartered banks might become members if they wished and met certain conditions. The Federal Reserve provided for a new, centralized system for maintaining bank reserves, for a new method of issuing currency, and made it possible for individual member banks to borrow from the Federal Reserve Banks. Most important of all, the new legislation put control of the nation's money supply into the hands of the Board of Governors of the Federal Reserve System.

Under the national banking system, banks had held reserves either in currency and coin in their own vaults or in the form of deposit claims on other banks. Under the new system, member banks were required to maintain reserves in the form of deposits at the Federal Reserve Bank in their district. These reserve deposits must be equal to a certain percentage of a bank's demand liabilities and a lower percentage of time and saving deposits (see Table 3-1). The reserve deposit which a bank must hold is called its "required reserve." Reserve balances over and above those required by the law are referred to as "excess reserves." The Board of Governors has the power to vary the reserve requirement percentages within broad limits.

The banks which entered the system at its formation in 1914 met the reserve requirement by transferring currency and coin formerly held in their vaults to the Federal Reserve Banks, receiving deposit credit on the books of the Federal Reserve Banks.[1]

Banks also acquired reserves as a result of gold imports to the United States. A considerable amount of foreign gold was sold in the United States during and after World War I, and even larger amounts during the 1930's.

Table 3-1 REQUIRED RESERVES, JANUARY 1, 1971
(Per cent of Deposits)

	Reserve City Banks		Country Banks	
	Under $5 Million	Over $5 Million	Under $5 Million	Over $5 Million
Against demand-deposits	17	17½	12½	13
Savings deposits	3	3	3	3
Other time deposits	3	5	3	5

Federal Reserve Lending to Member Banks

A member bank which finds it difficult to meet its reserve requirements may borrow from the Federal Reserve Bank in its district. In order to borrow, a member bank must deposit U.S. securities or promissory notes of business firms to which the bank has made loans. The Federal Reserve Bank extends the loans by giving the bank credit in its reserve deposit account. In effect, the Federal Reserve Bank exchanges liabilities with the member bank. The member bank owes the Federal Reserve Bank because of the loan, but the Federal Reserve Bank owes the member bank as well because the reserve "deposit" is a claim against the Federal Reserve Bank.

The member banks that borrow from Federal Reserve Banks pay interest on their indebtedness. The rate of interest charged them is called *discount*

[1] Since 1961, banks have been permitted to count vault cash as part of their required reserves.

rate. By varying this rate the Federal Reserve Bank can make it more profitable or less profitable for banks to borrow.

In addition, the Federal Reserve Banks limit the amount of member-bank borrowing by warning banks that borrow too much, too often, or for too long a time. The privilege of borrowing is very seldom refused, but without any formal action the Federal Reserve Banks make member banks aware that they are overworking the discount privilege.

Note Issue

The Federal Reserve Banks issue the bulk of our currency. Federal Reserve Notes, issued in denominations of $1 to $1,000, are liabilities of the Federal Reserve Bank. They are legal tender for all debts and tax payments. In order to issue notes, a Federal Reserve Bank must deposit with the Treasury at least 25 cents in gold for every dollar of notes issued and 75 cents in government securities or suitable promissory notes of business firms.

The Federal Reserve Banks could, if they wished, put their notes into circulation by using them to buy government securities or paying them out to member banks when making loans. In practice, however, the Federal Reserve Banks issue notes to banks in much the same way as a bank pays out cash to its customers. When a member bank's customer requests currency, the bank pays it out from currency held in its vault—and, of course, charges (reduces) the deposit account of the person making the withdrawal. If the bank feels that it has insufficient currency in its vault, it requests more from its Federal Reserve Bank. The Federal Reserve Bank in turn pays out the notes to the bank and charges (reduces) the reserve deposit account of the member bank.

This arrangement met the currency problems that had arisen under the national banking system. In the fall when business usually expands and banks have to pay out a great deal of currency, member banks obtain additional currency from Federal Reserve Banks. After the first of the year, bank customers usually deposit more currency than they take out. Member banks then return the excess currency to Federal Reserve Banks. Thus the seasonal shortage of currency which plagued the national banking system is eliminated.

Until 1933 the status of Federal Reserve Notes was essentially the same as that of the bank notes issued by private banks. They were liabilities of the Federal Reserve Bank issuing them and were a promise to pay "lawful money"—gold coin or Treasury currency—on demand. After 1933 the Federal Reserve Banks were no longer obligated to pay out gold coin in exchange for their notes. But their legal-tender status, together with the fact that everyone was used to them, insured their continued acceptability.

Federal Reserve Security Purchases

Banks gain reserves from gold imports when currency is deposited and when they borrow from the Federal Reserve; they lose reserves when currency in circulation increases, when gold is exported, or when member banks repay debts to Federal Reserve Banks. In discussing the national banking system, we mentioned that banking panics were caused in part at least by the difficulties faced by banks in meeting a loss of reserves due to an increased demand for currency or a loss of gold. The ability of Federal Banks to lend to member banks absorbs these disturbances. But it is not necessary for the Federal Reserve System to be passive in this matter. The Federal Reserve need not wait for banks to borrow. It can actively defend the banking system from disturbances caused by gains or losses of reserves associated with the flow of currency and gold. The Federal Reserve can provide the banking system as a whole with additional reserves by purchasing government securities from the public.

The process works as follows: the Federal Reserve Bank orders securities from a government-bond dealer who will in turn buy them from someone else. The Federal Reserve Bank pays with a check on itself. The person selling the securities will deposit the check in a commercial bank which will (a) credit the customer's deposit account, and (b) send the check to the Federal Reserve Bank for credit in its reserve deposit account (see p. 29 for balance-sheet entries).

As a result of its purchase of securities, the Federal Reserve Bank has increased its own assets and its own liabilities, in the form of member-bank reserve balances. At the same time, member banks have increased their liabilities to customers (customer deposits) and have gained an asset in the form of an increased claim against the Federal Reserve Bank. The Federal Reserve Bank has created additional reserve balances in just the same way that it can manufacture notes with a printing press.

The process of increasing bank reserves by buying securities can be reversed. The Federal Reserve Banks usually buy securities in the fall months and sell them after the turn of the year when a large amount of currency returns to banks with the seasonal fall in retail sales. The sale of securities by the Federal Reserve Banks has exactly the opposite effect of a security purchase. Thus it is possible for the Federal Reserve Banks to control the volume of bank reserves at will. Federal Reserve purchases and sales of United States securities are called *open-market operations.*

The Federal Reserve System can and frequently does use its powers to buy and sell securities to keep bank reserves constant—selling securities to offset gains in reserves from other sources and buying to offset losses from other sources. But if it wishes, it can use those same powers to make a net addition to the supply of bank reserves. This ability to control bank reserves by the use of open-market operations is one of the Federal Reserve System's most important powers.

DEPOSIT EXPANSION UNDER THE FEDERAL RESERVE SYSTEM

In Chapter 2 we showed how a deposit of coin in a commercial bank would lead to the creation of a total amount of deposits several times the amount of the original deposit. American banks still operate on the *fractional reserve* principle, and deposit expansion still occurs in the way in which it was described in Chapter 2. Nowadays, of course, banks use Federal Reserve facilities for clearing checks, but that is only a mechanical difference. And reserve requirements are not a matter of judgment for the individual banker but are set by the Board of Governors.

The most important difference between modern banking and early deposit banking is the nature of the funds which constitute bank reserves. In the banking system described in Chapter 2, banks held reserves in coin or currency. They got those reserves in the first instance when individuals or business firms brought in coin or currency which had been hoarded or used in hand-to-hand transactions or which had been imported.

The original deposits which provide banks with reserves today consist of checks on Federal Reserve Banks. Of course, people do deposit currency in banks, but they also withdraw it, and on balance the withdrawals of currency exceed the deposits.

Let us suppose that the Board of Governors decides that an expansion of the money supply is appropriate. It instructs the Federal Reserve Bank of New York to buy $1 million worth of U.S. securities. Through a bond dealer in New York, the bank buys the securities from some individual or corporation, paying with a check on itself. The seller deposits the check in some commercial bank (bank *A*). Bank *A* will credit the seller's account and return the check to the Federal Reserve Bank for credit in its reserve account.

Bank *A* has now increased its deposit liabilities by $1 million and its assets in the form of reserve deposits at the Federal Reserve Bank by the same amount. The Federal Reserve Bank has increased its deposit liabilities (member-bank reserve deposits) by $1 million and its assets, in the form of U.S. securities, by an equal amount.

The transaction has resulted in the creation of a million dollars of demand deposits and a million dollars of additional bank reserves. No one is richer because of it. The public holds a million dollars more demand deposits but it holds a million dollars less U.S. securities. This transaction and the others following it are summarized in the numbered steps below:

1. When the Federal Reserve Bank purchases government securities, a member bank gains reserves because the seller of the securities deposits the

check drawn on the Federal Reserve in his bank (bank *A*) which then sends the check to its Federal Reserve Bank and receives credit in its reserve account. The changes in the balance sheet of bank *A* and the Federal Reserve Banks would be represented thus:

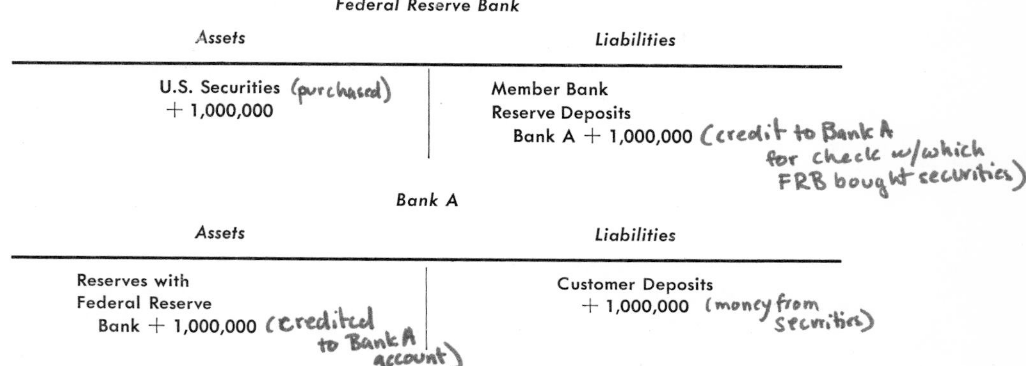

Federal Reserve Bank

Assets	*Liabilities*
U.S. Securities + 1,000,000	Member Bank Reserve Deposits Bank A + 1,000,000

Bank A

Assets	*Liabilities*
Reserves with Federal Reserve Bank + 1,000,000	Customer Deposits + 1,000,000

The story doesn't end there, however. Bank *A* has increased its reserves and deposits by $1 million but its *required* reserve has increased by only $150,000, assuming a reserve requirement of 15 per cent. It therefore gained *excess* reserves of $850,000.

Bank *A* is now in a position to expand its earning assets by making additional loans or buying securities. It can make loans or buy securities in an amount equal to its excess reserve ($850,000). We will see in a moment why it wouldn't be safe to go beyond that amount. If business is expanding, bank *A* may make additional loans of $850,000. It will make the loan by crediting the deposit account of the borrower, receiving a promissory note from the borrower in exchange. Bank *A* will have added to its deposit liabilities by $850,000 and to its assets in loans by an equal amount.

2. Additional deposits are created when the bank with excess reserves makes loans by crediting borrowers' deposit accounts for the amount of the loan. The changes in bank *A*'s balance sheet are shown below:

Bank A

Assets	*Liabilities*
Loans + 850,000	Borrower Deposits + 850,000

This is the first stage of deposit expansion by commercial banks. Taking the original action of the Federal Reserve together with bank *A*'s action in making loans, commercial banks and the Federal Reserve System have added $1,850,000 to demand deposits.

3. The Federal Reserve purchase, together with the loans made by bank *A*, has increased deposits by a total of $1,850,000, loans by $850,000, and member bank reserves by $1,000,000. The changed position of bank *A* as a result of the two sets of transactions is shown thus:

Bank A

Assets		*Liabilities*	
Reserves with Federal Reserve Bank	+ 1,000,000	Initial Deposits	+ 1,000,000
		Stage 1 Deposits	+ 850,000
Loans	+ 850,000	Total	+ 1,850,000

Of course, things won't stay that way very long. The business firms who borrowed from bank *A* did so because they wanted to buy something. The borrowers wanted to buy raw materials or equipment. Once they get the loan, they will buy what they need and pay for it by check. The businesses receiving the checks *might* be customers of bank *A*, but since there are 13,000 banks in the United States, that is not very likely. The checks written by those who borrowed from bank *A* will be deposited in other banks. The other banks will send the checks to a Federal Reserve Bank for credit in their reserve accounts. The Federal Reserve Bank will charge bank *A*'s reserve account and return the checks to bank *A*. Bank *A* will, of course, charge the borrowers' accounts when it gets the checks.

Notice that these transactions leave the total of bank reserves unchanged but pass the reserves on from bank *A* to other banks.

4. When borrowers write checks, deposits and reserves are transferred from bank *A* to other banks. Total deposits and reserves remain unchanged. The changes in bank balance sheets are shown below:

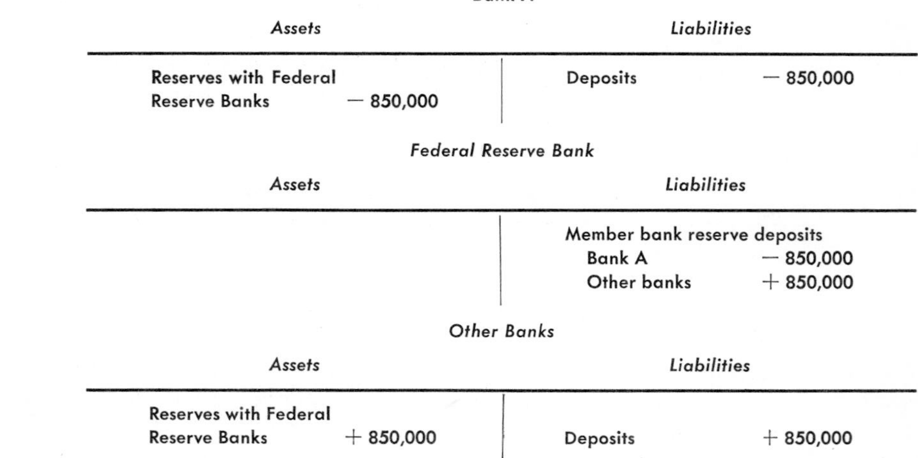

Bank A

Assets		*Liabilities*	
Reserves with Federal Reserve Banks	− 850,000	Deposits	− 850,000

Federal Reserve Bank

Assets		*Liabilities*	
		Member bank reserve deposits	
		Bank A	− 850,000
		Other banks	+ 850,000

Other Banks

Assets		*Liabilities*	
Reserves with Federal Reserve Banks	+ 850,000	Deposits	+ 850,000

We now see why bank *A* could not expand loans by more than the $850,000 of excess reserves. The bank knew that the borrowers were going to draw checks against the deposit credit given them when the loans were made. It knew that the only safe procedure is to assume that for every dollar of deposits created by lending, a dollar of reserves will be lost to another bank.

After all these transactions, bank *A* winds up just meeting its required reserve. It has a million dollars more in deposit liabilities than it had at the start. Its reserve deposit is up by $150,000 as required by law, and it has increased its loans by $850,000. The final position of bank *A* is shown below:

Bank A

Assets		*Liabilities*	
Reserves with Federal Reserve Bank	+ 150,000	Deposits	+ 1,000,000
Loans	+ 850,000		

Now notice the position of "other" banks shown in step 4. It's exactly like the position of bank *A* in step 1 except that the amounts involved in step 4 are only 85 per cent of those in step 1.

They are now ready to generate a second stage of commercial bank deposit expansion. These "other," or "stage-2," banks have excess reserves of $722,500 (85% of $850,000). They can make loans in that amount, creating an equivalent amount of deposits in the process.

5. Banks which gained reserves from bank *A* (step 4 above) expand loans and deposits. The bookkeeping entries resulting from those transactions are shown thus:

Stage-2 Banks

Assets		*Liabilities*	
Loans	+ 722,500	Borrowers' Deposits	+ 722,500

6. The banking system has now generated a total of $2,572,500 in new deposits, $1,572,500 of loans. The change to date for the whole banking system is shown thus:

All Commercial Banks

Assets		*Liabilities*	
Reserves with Federal Reserve Bank	+ 1,000,000	Deposits	
		Initial	+ 1,000,000
Loans		Stage 1	+ 850,000
Stage 1	850,000	Stage 2	+ 722,500
Stage 2	722,500		2,572,500
Total Loans	+ 1,572,500	Total Deposits	+ 2,572,500

The stage-2 banks will lose deposits and reserves when borrowers spend the proceeds. The stage-2 banks will be left with deposits of \$850,000 and reserves of \$127,500, which leaves them with a reserve of just 15 per cent.

The \$722,500 of deposits created by the stage-2 banks and an equivalent amount of reserves will have passed to a third group of banks. They require a reserve of \$108,375 and have excess reserves of \$614,125.

The whole process can then be repeated by these stage-3 banks. And, of course, when that stage is completed, the process can be repeated again. Indeed, it can go on indefinitely. But the amount of new loans and deposits generated at each step of the process becomes progressively smaller. In fact, each step is 85 per cent the size of the preceding one. The banks at each stage can create new deposits equal to 85 per cent of the reserves they gain as a result of deposit creation by banks in the preceding stage. The other 15 per cent is tied up in required reserves against the deposits transferred from other banks.

The whole process is summed up in the table below.

Banks at each stage received deposits and reserves (column 1) from other banks (in the case of bank *A*, as a result of the Federal Reserve Bank's action; after that, each bank receives deposits and reserves because other banks have made loans against which checks were drawn and deposited in the banks in question). Only 15 per cent of the reserves received are required against the deposits received (column 2). The remainder of the reserves received are excess reserves (column 3). Banks with excess reserves make loans and investments (column 4), creating equal amounts of deposits (column 5). The connection between excess reserves, making loans, and creating deposits is indicated by the arrows from column 3 to column 4, and

Deposit Expansion (in dollars)

	1 Deposits and Reserves Received from Others	2 Reserve Required against Deposits from Others	3 Excess Reserve 1-2	4 Loans and Invest-ments	5 Deposits Created	6 Reserve and Deposits Lost to Others	7 Reserve Remain-ing	8 Deposit Remain-ing
Bank A	1,000,000	150,000	850,000	850,000	850,000	850,000	150,000	1,000,000
Stage 2	850,000	127,500	722,500	722,500	722,500	722,500	127,500	850,000
Stage 3	722,500	108,375	614,125	614,125	614,125	614,125	108,375	722,500

from column 4 to column 5. The deposits thus created are lost to others when borrowers write checks. The arrows from column 6 to column 1 indicate that the deposits and reserves lost by one group of banks are gained by another. Column 7 and column 8 indicate that each bank is left with reserves which are just 15 per cent of its deposits, as required.

The cumulative results of these stages are shown in the following table:

Cumulative Deposit Expansion (thousands of dollars)

	1	2	3	4	5	6	7
Banks	*Deposits Created*	*Total So Far*	*Loans and Invest-ments Made*	*Total So Far*	*Total Reserves*	*Required Reserves against Deposits Created*	*Total So Far*
Federal Reserve	$1,000	$1,000	—	—	$1,000	$150	$ 150
Stage 1	850	1,850	850	850	1,000	128	278
Stage 2	722	2,572	722	1,572	1,000	108	386
Stage 3	614	3,186	614	2,186	1,000	92	478
Stage 4	522	3,708	522	2,708	1,000	78	556
Stage 5	444	4,152	444	3,152	1,000	67	623
Stage 6	377	4,529	377	3,529	1,000	57	680
Stage 7	320	4,849	320	3,849	1,000	48	728
Stage 8	272	5,121	272	4,121	1,000	41	769
Stage 9	231	5,352	231	4,352	1,000	34	803
Stage 10	197	5,549	197	4,549	1,000	30	833
Stage 20	46	6,448	46	5,448	1,000	7	961
Final	—	6,667	—	5,667	1,000	—	1,000

The first column shows the deposits created at each step of the process, including the initial security purchase by the Federal Reserve System. Except for the first entry, the column is the same as column 5 in the preceding chart. The second column shows the sum of the deposits created up to and including the completion of each stage. The next two columns show the loans and investments made at each stage of the process and their sum. The final two columns show the reserves required against the deposits required at each stage and the sum to date.

You can see that the total deposits created grows larger and larger as the process continues, but the *additional* amount created is growing smaller and smaller. At the same time, more and more of the initial $1,000 of new reserves is being absorbed into required reserves. Also notice that the ratio of total required reserves (column 6) to total deposits created (column 2) is always just 15 per cent.

Eventually all the $1,000,000 of additional reserves will be absorbed into required reserves, and $1,000,000 will equal 15 per cent of the total deposits created. So $\frac{\$1{,}000{,}000}{.15} =$ total deposits created. Or total deposits created $= \frac{\$1{,}000{,}000}{.15} = \$6{,}667{,}000$.

If you examine this same table, you can see how total deposits approach that limit. At the end of the first 10 steps, $5,549 worth of deposits has been created. At the end of the first 20 steps, $6,448 worth of new money has been created.

The process is shown graphically in Fig. 3-1. More generally, we can tell the amount of deposits created by any given amount of new reserves at any required reserve ratio by the formula

$$\text{Total deposits created} = \frac{\text{New reserves}}{\text{Reserve ratio}}$$

The Federal Reserve System by buying securities can set in motion at any time the multiple expansion process we have just described. Since it can also sell securities, it can reverse the whole process if it wishes.

Suppose the Federal Reserve Bank of New York sells $1 million worth of securities to a large corporation. The buyer pays with a check on bank *A*. The Federal Reserve Bank charges (reduces) bank *A*'s reserve account by $1 million, and bank *A* reduces the customer's account when it receives the check. Bank deposits and reserves have both been reduced by $1 million. But bank *A*'s required reserve has declined by only $150,000. If it had no excess reserves before, it now has a reserve deficit of $850,000. Bank *A* will try to make up the deficit by selling securities. If bank *A* sells securities to customers of another bank, it will gain reserves which the other bank loses. The second bank will now have to deal with its loss of reserves. See if you can follow through the remaining steps of the process of deposit contraction.

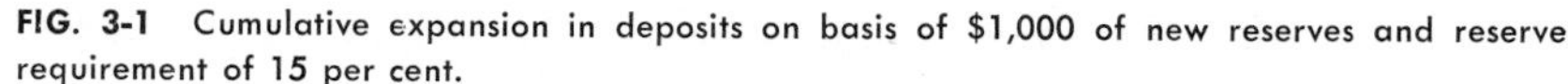
FIG. 3-1 Cumulative expansion in deposits on basis of $1,000 of new reserves and reserve requirement of 15 per cent.

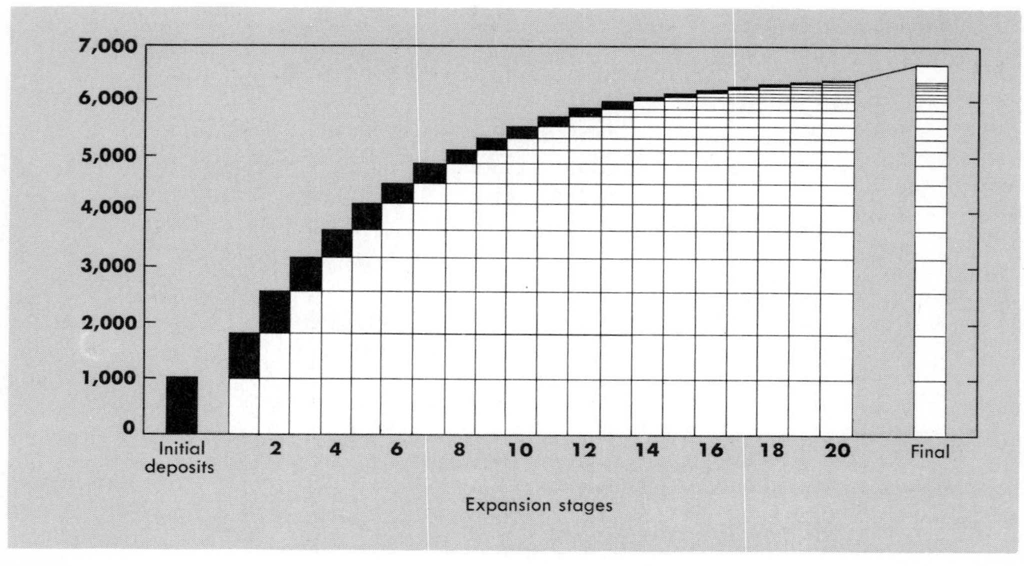

Varying Reserve Requirements

The Board of Governors has another powerful instrument for controlling the money supply and the volume of bank loans and investments. The Board can change the required ratios of reserves to deposits. The power to vary reserve requirements was first granted in 1933. Currently, the Board is empowered to set reserve requirements with the following limits:

On demand deposits	
Reserve and central reserve city banks	10 to 22 per cent
Country banks	7 to 14 per cent
On time deposits for all banks	3 to 6 per cent

The amount of demand deposits which can be supported by a given volume of reserves is $\frac{1}{\text{Required reserve rate}} \times$ amount of reserves.

The amount of demand deposits which can be supported by a given volume of reserves is twice as large when the reserve ratio is 10 per cent as when it is 20 per cent. Thus even small changes in required reserve percentages can have a substantial effect on the volume of bank deposits. A change in the required reserve ratio from 20 per cent to 19 per cent would increase potential total demand deposits by 1/20, or 5 per cent.

The reaction to the change in reserve requirements follows a series of steps, as does the response to an open-market operation. When reserve requirements are lowered, a portion of existing bank holdings of required reserves becomes excess reserves. For example, suppose bank reserves were $20 billion, demand deposits $100 billion, and the required reserve ratio 20 per cent. A reduction of the required reserve ratio to 19 per cent would reduce required reserves to $19 billion, leaving banks with $1 billion of excess reserves. Banks can make loans or buy investments to the tune of $1 billion, creating $1 billion of new demand deposits in the process. The creation of $1 billion of new deposits will absorb $190 million of the excess reserves into required reserves, but leave $810 million of excess reserves. After that, the process will continue in the same way as in an open-market operation.

THREE INSTRUMENTS FOR CONTROLLING THE MONEY SUPPLY

The volume of bank deposits which can be created by the banking system depends on (1) the volume of bank reserves, and (2) the average required reserve ratio. The Federal Reserve System controls the second factor directly. By means of open-market operations, the system can control the volume of unborrowed reserves. The system exercises control over borrowed reserves by controlling the discount rate charged member banks and by warning banks which borrow too much for too long.

By *variable reserve requirements, open-market operations,* and the *discount rate* the Federal Reserve System can place an upper limit on the volume of demand deposits. Controlling the upper limit of bank deposits is nearly the same thing as controlling the actual volume of deposits, since it is ordinarily profitable for banks to buy securities or make loans when they have excess reserves.

MONETARY POLICY AND ECONOMIC ACTIVITY

By controlling the money supply, the Federal Reserve System can exert a strong influence on the course of economic activity. In recessions everyone wants to encourage investment expenditures to check the decline in aggregate income and expenditures. The Federal Reserve System contributes to that objective by using its powers over the money supply. Federal Reserve action and its effect can be summarized as follows:

1. The Federal Reserve System can: (a) reduce discount rates, (b) buy securities in the open market, and (c) reduce reserve requirements.
2. Banks use their increased resources to buy bonds and at the same time become more willing to lend to businesses or to lend on mortgages to home-builders.
3. When banks start to buy bonds, their prices tend to rise, reducing the interest rates (yields) on bonds.
4. Credit is therefore cheaper and more readily available, which encourages businesses to invest and makes it easier and cheaper to buy or build houses. Investment expenditures tend to rise.
5. The "multiplier" effects of increased investment expenditures lead to further increases in income and expenditures.

During booms, when inflation threatens, the Federal Reserve System may act in the opposite direction—to check the growth of expenditures by raising discount rates, selling in the open market, and raising reserve requirements. The whole sequence then works in the opposite direction.

This is a drastically oversimplified account of how Federal Reserve policy affects the economy. In the next chapter we will look more closely at the response of banks to changes in Federal Reserve policy. Then we can consider in Chapter 5 how the response of banks is communicated to the rest of the economy through its effects on financial institutions and other lenders and borrowers.

SUMMARY

In the preceding two chapters we traced the evolution of our monetary system from commodity money to pure debt money. At the same time, we documented the long struggle for control of the money supply. Metallic money, money supplied by unregulated private banks, and the national banking system all proved defective in one way or another.

The present system may be summarized as follows: (1) The bulk of our currency consists of Federal Reserve Notes, which are essentially the same as the private bank notes described earlier. However, the Federal Reserve Banks have a monopoly of note issue and Federal Reserve Notes are not for practical purposes convertible into anything else. Banks always have to be prepared to pay out notes to depositors who ask for them, but banks can always get additional notes from Federal Reserve Banks. When a Federal Reserve Bank supplies notes to a member bank, it charges that bank's reserve account. (2) Over two thirds of our money supply consists of demand balances at commercial banks. The total volume of demand deposits depends on the volume of reserves and the legal reserve ratios. The Federal Reserve System controls legal reserve ratios directly. It can control the volume of reserves by open-market operations and by changing the discount rate. By the use of these three instruments, the system therefore controls the volume of demand deposits.

This system is free of the mechanical defects which plagued earlier monetary systems. The money supply does not depend on the chance discovery of gold, nor on the seasonal swings in currency demands, nor is it subject to the wild gyrations of a free banking regime.

The Modern Commercial Bank

CHAPTER FOUR

So far we have been concerned with the process by which banks create money. Now it's time to take a closer look at the practical operation of modern commercial banks. This is not such an easy task because commercial banking is a large and complex industry. It has come a long way from the days of the wildcat banks.

There are over 13,000 banks in the United States, varying in size from banks like the Chase Manhattan Bank and the Bank of America, with over $10 billion of assets, to banks with less than $1 million of assets. The nature and scope of their activities also vary widely. Some large city banks are mainly banks for business, with few individual accounts. Others have tried to develop their retail businesses with individuals by establishing branches, extending banking hours, and in other ways. Commercial banking is a major industry in terms of employment and value of services produced. Over 700,000 people were employed by commercial banks in 1963, and the estimated value of the services of banks was over $7 billion.

PROBLEMS OF BANK MANAGEMENT

Banks, like other private businesses, are operated for profit. The basic source of bank earnings is the fact that a bank can earn a higher rate of interest on its assets—loans and investments—than it must pay to its depositors. The excess of interest received over interest paid can be used to pay the cost of operating the bank, and what remains is profit to the bank's stockholders.[1]

Banks do not pay interest on demand deposits, but to induce businesses and households to hold deposits without receiving interest, banks give their services free or at less than full cost. Bank service charges do not cover the full cost of check transfers, record-keeping, rendering statements, and so on. The difference is covered by the net earnings on loans and investments.

Although banks do not pay interest on checking accounts, they usually do pay interest on time (or savings) deposits. While demand deposits can be transferred from one person to another by check, time deposits cannot. The owner of a savings deposit must present his pass book at the bank to withdraw his funds. He can take away currency or get a bank check, which he can deposit in his checking account.

Because of the inconvenience of withdrawing funds in person, most people use savings accounts only when they expect to keep their funds on deposit for some time. As a result, the amount of savings deposits held by a bank does not fluctuate much, and a bank can invest in mortgages or other long-term assets which usually earn more interest than short-term loans.

Commercial banks are in competition for savings deposits with mutual savings banks and savings-and-loan associations. In the last few years there has been intense competition among these institutions, and interest rates on savings accounts have increased while depositors have been wooed with advertising campaigns.

A bank naturally wishes to invest in assets yielding the highest net return. But in making its investment choices it must be constantly aware of its obligation to its depositors. It must be prepared at all times to meet its legal reserve requirement by maintaining the required deposit balance at the Federal Reserve Bank. It must maintain enough vault cash to meet the day-to-day changes in the flow of currency into and out of the bank. In addition, it must have in cash or in assets which can be readily sold, enough funds to meet deposit withdrawals. Finally, it must conduct its whole investment policy in such a way as to keep losses from bad debts or unsuccessful investments at a very low level.

Every investment involves some risk of loss. And investments offering high returns are generally more risky and less easily turned into cash (hence are less "liquid") than those offering low returns. Bank managements must continually balance the need for safety and liquidity against their desire for higher earnings. A bank which never takes any risk of loss on an investment

[1] The interest received by a bank is not, of course, all available to cover the costs of servicing deposit accounts. Though they are generally conservative investors, banks take some losses on their loans and investments. Moreover, to avoid losses, a bank must pay the cost of credit investigation, security analysis, and so on. In the case of mortgage and consumer loans, there are substantial costs involved in receiving monthly payments, returning statements, and checking on delinquent borrowers.

cannot earn enough to cover its costs. But a bank which gambles on high-return investments may fail.

BANK FAILURES

Bank failures have been rare in recent decades. The problems of maintaining enough liquid assets to meet deposit withdrawals and of avoiding excessive losses on loans and investments may not look very serious these days. But we have only to look at the record of the 1920's and the early 1930's to see that they are very real problems. During the prosperous 1920's, banks failed at a rate of over 500 a year. Most of the failing banks were very small, and they held only about 3 per cent of total deposits. With the onset of the depression, the failure rate rose sharply; 1,300 banks failed in 1930, 2,200 in 1931, and 1,400 in 1932. By the beginning of 1933, several state governors closed all the banks in their states, and in March, 1933, President Roosevelt declared a national "bank holiday." All the banks were closed for a time. Most of them were then permitted to reopen and the public was assured that those licensed to reopen were solvent.

The banks which failed during the 1920's and in the early period of the depression had, for the most part, been badly managed. They had failed to maintain enough assets which could be readily sold to meet withdrawals of deposits. Some had taken heavy losses because they had placed all their eggs in one basket—e.g., loans to local farmers. When farm income in the area declined, the bank was bound to fail. Some large city banks had invested heavily in doubtful securities during the boom of the 'twenties.

The failure of large numbers of badly managed banks finally undermined public confidence in the whole banking system. Once the public became really frightened and began to withdraw deposits *en masse,* the strong fell with the weak. Perfectly solvent banks and banks with cash and readily salable assets sufficient to meet any normal contingency could not meet the panic demand for cash.

BANK REGULATION AND DEPOSIT INSURANCE

The disastrous experiences of the early 1930's produced a number of important changes in the banking system.

First of all, the disaster itself swept away a large number of very small, badly managed banks. The number of banks in the United States had risen from about 9,000 in 1900 to over 30,000 in 1920. It had already fallen to 24,000 by 1929 and by 1933 was reduced to about 15,000. The reduction in the number of very small banks did a good deal to strengthen the banking system.

Second, regulatory standards were generally tightened. Banks have always been regulated, of course, but they have been regulated more closely since 1933.

Every bank must obtain a charter either from the federal government or from the state in which it operates. To obtain a charter, the incorporators must provide a certain minimum amount of capital and demonstrate that the officers and directors are competent to operate a bank and have records of financial honesty. In addition, they must show that there is some need for additional banking services in the area in which they propose to operate.

Regulation does not stop there, however. The National Banking Act and state legislation impose certain limitations on the investments which banks can make. For example: a national bank cannot buy common stock (except of other banks), or lend an amount equal to more than 10 per cent of its capital and surplus to a single customer. The banking authorities regularly examine the banks in their jurisdiction, not only to audit their books but also to check the adherence of each bank's management to "sound banking practice" as conceived by the examining authorities. Bank examiners may reprimand banks which buy low-quality bonds, or acquire too many loans which go into default or have to be repeatedly renewed. They require banks to have sufficient capital and surplus to absorb any losses which the bank may take on its loans or investments and so protect the depositors from loss. Any bank which continuously flouts the recommendations of examiners may have its charter suspended, although, in practice, few ever do.

The reduction in the number of banks and the tightening of regulations have greatly reduced the incidence of bank failures. But the experience of the 'thirties showed that even sound, well-managed banks can fail if their depositors become sufficiently frightened. To solve that problem, a system of deposit insurance was developed. In 1934 the Federal Deposit Insurance Corporation was established. Over 97 per cent of all commercial banks, holding 99 per cent of commercial bank deposits, are insured by the F.D.I.C. Each bank pays an annual premium of ¼ per cent of deposits, and in return the F.D.I.C. insures all deposit accounts up to $15,000 per account. In the event of a bank failure, the F.D.I.C. takes over the bank's assets and pays off the depositors. Runs on insured banks have become a rarity—a tribute to the public's confidence in deposit insurance.

MANAGING BANK FUNDS

Deposit insurance and bank regulation protect depositors from loss as a result of panic or poor management or both. But the management of the individual bank is still responsible for maintaining the bank's solvency, for maintaining the bank's ability to meet deposit withdrawals, and for earning enough from loans and investments to cover the bank's operating costs and earn a profit for the stockholders.

The first task of a bank management is to meet the legal reserve requirements and to be prepared to meet deposit withdrawals. Banks must be prepared to meet their customers' requests for currency without question and must therefore keep coin and currency in their vaults.

Banks must also be prepared to deal with withdrawals by check. In a banking system in which even the largest bank has only a small percentage of total deposits, individual banks find their deposits fluctuating continuously. Small rural banks are subject to sharp seasonal fluctuations, whereas larger banks are subject to erratic changes in deposits as a result of the operations of their corporate customers. For example, a large corporation may accumulate several million dollars in a New York bank, then pay it all away in dividend checks, most of which will be deposited elsewhere. Or a corporation will raise several million dollars by selling securities and deposit the proceeds in its principal account. In these operations, one bank's deposit gain is another's loss, but each bank must make its own adjustment to the change.

When a bank suffers a net loss of deposits, its account at the Federal Reserve will be charged that amount. If it formerly held exactly the required reserve, it will now have less than the required reserve. For its deposit at the Federal Reserve will be down $1 for every $1 withdrawn, whereas its required reserve is down only $.15, if the required reserve ratio is 15 per cent. It therefore has a deficit in its reserve account of $.85 per dollar of deposit loss. To be prepared to meet deposit losses, therefore, a bank must either carry deposits at the Federal Reserve in excess of the legal requirement or be prepared to replenish its account at the Federal Reserve Bank very quickly. Many small banks do carry excess reserves as a normal procedure. But, since deposits at the Federal Reserve earn no interest, that is a relatively costly way of preparing for deposit withdrawals.

In addition to their vault cash and deposit with the Federal Reserve Bank, most banks maintain deposits at other banks. Banks in small towns and cities maintain balances with banks in larger cities. They may draw on those balances to meet deposit withdrawals. In addition, they receive many kinds of services, such as investment advice, safe keeping of securities, and processing of checks, from their city correspondents.

Vault cash, excess reserves, and deposits with other banks are one line of defense against deposit losses. In addition, most banks try to prepare for deposit withdrawals, without losing too much interest, by investing in securities which can be readily sold with no risk of loss. For this purpose the ideal instrument is a security of the federal government due to mature in a short time.

There is no risk of default on these securities, and if they are due to mature shortly their prices cannot fluctuate much. There is an active, well-organized market in these securities, and the cost of buying and selling them is very low. By holding securities of this type, a bank can earn interest and still be prepared to meet deposit losses. If deposit losses do occur, it sells part of its short-dated federal securities to other banks or their customers. It will receive payment by check on another bank, and, when it sends that check to its Federal Reserve Bank it will have its account credited, thus offsetting the loss of deposit at the Federal Reserve Bank which occurred earlier.

A bank suffering from deposit losses may also borrow from its Federal Reserve Bank. Assuming that the bank is not already in debt, it can obtain a loan from its Federal Reserve Bank without much question, pledging government securities against the loan. The Federal Reserve Bank will credit the commercial bank with the amount of the loan, thus replenishing its reserves.

Choice Among Alternative Reserve Adjustments

Individual banks are constantly gaining or losing deposits and must take frequent action to adjust their reserve positions. A bank which loses reserves must choose whether to draw on its excess reserves (if any), draw on balances with correspondent banks, sell securities, or borrow from its Federal Reserve Bank.

In choosing whether to borrow from the Federal Reserve or to sell securities, a bank considers the relative costs. If the discount rate is above the going interest rate on short-term government securities, the bank will find it cheaper to sell securities than to borrow. If the discount rate is below the rate on short-term securities, it will pay to borrow. However, banks must limit their Federal Reserve borrowing. Even if a bank finds it profitable to borrow from the Federal Reserve for an extended period, it cannot always do so. A bank which borrows too much for too long will find itself subject to pressure from Federal Reserve officials to get out of debt.[2]

Once a bank has met its legal reserve requirements, provided an adequate supply of vault cash, placed sufficient deposits with correspondents, and acquired enough highly liquid securities to meet possible deposit losses, it may use the balance of its funds to make loans or to buy other securities.

In placing its funds, a bank must not only conform to the legal restrictions mentioned above but also must confine itself to loans and securities of the highest quality. A bank cannot afford to gamble. Subject to that qualification, banks naturally prefer to invest their funds in assets promising the highest yields.

The nominal interest rate, however, is not always the ruling consideration. Interest charged on consumer installment loans is much higher than on other loans or securities, but the interest earned is partly offset by the costs involved in those loans. State and local securities are a better investment for a bank than corporate securities, even though nominal interest

[2] For very short periods, a bank can borrow excess reserves of another bank. There is a telephone market in "federal funds," with which banks can meet reserve shortages for a few days. The interest rate in this market, the federal funds rate, is a sensitive indicator of bank credit conditions.

rates are lower, because the interest on state and local securities is tax free. Finally, and perhaps most important, the net gain from making loans to deposit customers is only partially measured by the interest received on the loan.

Business Loans and Customer Relationships

The relationship between a bank and its business deposit customers is a continuing one, not a series of isolated transactions. A business firm keeps deposits with a bank for years at a time, and the bank is able to earn interest as a result. The bank in turn performs services such as processing wage and dividend checks without charge. It may also supply financial advice, credit information, and other incidental services. If the customer's average deposit balance is more than sufficient to cover the average cost of the services provided by the bank, the customer is valuable to the bank. When such a customer asks for a loan, the bank is very much inclined to accommodate him if it can possibly do so. The bank feels that if it refuses loans to a good (i.e., profitable) deposit customer, the customer is likely to take the first opportunity to establish a new banking connection. Of course, a customer who keeps an average balance of $10,000 cannot expect to borrow a million dollars. There has to be some relationship between the size and profitability of a customer's balance and the size of the loan he can expect to get. But subject to that condition, and when the customer's financial prospects justify the loan, banks give first priority to the loan requests of good deposit customers in allocating their funds. When loan demand is increasing more rapidly than deposits, a bank will be prepared to sell off securities, even at a loss, to accommodate its good-customer loan requests.

However, banks whose loan demand fluctuates over the business cycle try to avoid having to sell securities at a loss to accommodate loan demand. When business is poor and demand for loans is low, they invest part of their resources in relatively short-term securities, even though they could get a higher yield on longer-term assets. During an upsurge in the business cycle, the short-term securities bought during the slump will mature or can be sold with little loss and the proceeds used to increase loans to customers.

Consumer Loans

Loans to individuals—personal loans or installment credit connected with the purchase of durable goods—do not ordinarily involve an important customer relationship of the type described above. People who take installment credit do not ordinarily have large bank accounts. However, these loans generally give banks a better return than almost any other kind of asset.

Most banks are anxious to develop their consumer-loan business, since it is so profitable. They have done this by engaging in advertising campaigns and acquiring branch offices. And, as bank-lending to consumers has grown, banks have built up special staffs and personnel to handle the business. Once a bank has built up a market position, it is reluctant to risk losing it by turning away business. When the demand for consumer loans expands, banks generally try to accommodate it—selling off securities if necessary. Thus the fluctuations in demand for consumer loans pose problems for bank managements similar to those caused by fluctuations in loans to business customers.

Other Bank Assets

The assets just mentioned are particularly important for an understanding of the cyclical changes in the distribution of bank assets. But banks have many other kinds of assets. They make many loans to business firms and to individuals whose deposits do not warrant a priority status.

In addition to their holdings of relatively short-term United States securities, banks hold large amounts of other bonds. They hold several billion worth of U.S. securities having more than 5 years to run, as well as a smaller amount of corporate securities. The tax-exempt securities of state and local governments have been very attractive to banks in recent years, and commercial banks hold about $60 billion worth of these bonds. Finally, banks with offices in suburban areas hold mortgage loans.

The amount a bank can invest in long-term bonds and mortgages depends mainly on three factors.

1. *The stability of its deposits.* If a bank's deposits do not fluctuate much, it needs a relatively small reserve of short-term securities to meet deposit withdrawals.
2. *The proportion of its assets absorbed by the loan requirements of the deposit customers.*
3. *The extent to which the bank has built up its consumer-loan business.*

When business and consumer-loan demands are expanding rapidly, banks acquire relatively few of these longer-term assets. During periods of business contraction, when bank reserves are expanding rapidly, banks have used part of their increased resources to buy municipal securities, long-term United States securities, and mortgages.

COMPETITION FOR DEPOSITS

A bank with a given volume of deposits has to adjust the composition of its assets to meet the changing demand for business loans and to respond to changes in the relative yields of alternative investments. But when loan demand is strong and interest rates high, banks may also seek to increase their deposits.

Competition for Demand Deposits

Although banks are not permitted to pay interest on demand deposits, they can compete for them in a variety of ways. They service large business accounts without direct compensation and, as noted previously, they provide good deposit customers with loans. Banks seek to increase their consumer-demand deposits by advertising, opening new offices, keeping longer hours, and reducing service charges—"No service charge with $100 minimum balance." Many economists think that the banking system would operate more efficiently, with fewer offices and less advertising, if banks were permitted to compete for demand deposits by paying interest.

Since the total volume of deposits is limited by the available bank reserves, competition does not raise the total volume of demand deposits. Each bank's competitive efforts are aimed at increasing or maintaining its share of demand deposits.

Competition for Time Deposits

Banks can pay interest on time deposits, and during the last decade they have engaged in a competitive struggle with one another and with mutual savings banks and savings-and-loan associations. Competition for time deposits has frequently been restrained by Federal Reserve Board regulations. The Board establishes the maximum interest rates which banks may pay on time deposits of different amounts and maturities (regulation *Q*).

During the first decade after World War II, banks had very large volumes of relatively low-yielding government securities in their portfolios. They could meet the expanding demand for business loans by selling their securities, and they found it was more profitable to do so than to compete for time deposits. By the mid-1950's, however, banks had reduced their holdings of government securities and had begun to raise rates to attract time deposits. Their efforts were inhibited, however, by the regulation *Q* ceiling, which stayed at 2½ per cent until 1957. During the following decade, the regulation *Q* ceiling was raised several times and banks pushed their rate offers up to obtain more funds. They also developed a variety of new forms of time deposits for consumers (e.g., time certificates and special notice accounts, which enabled them to compete for the funds of some rate sensitive depositors without raising rates on all deposits; the ceiling rate on regular pass book accounts remained at 4 per cent until 1970). For business customers banks developed the "negotiable certificate of deposit." These certificates, with maturities of 30 days to a year, are sold in larger denominations—usually over $100,000—to corporations, and the corporate treasurer can sell them when he needs funds. These instruments are therefore direct competitors with Treasury bills and commercial paper.

Table 4–1 shows the phenomenal growth of time deposits in the early 1960's. It also shows how rapidly banks increased their share of total consumer time deposits. As banks raised their rates, the competing savings banks and savings-and-loan associations also raised theirs; but the interest earnings of the latter did not permit them to keep pace, and the spread of bank interest rates over thrift institution rates narrowed.

Table 4-1 TIME DEPOSITS AND SAVINGS ACCOUNTS (Billions of dollars)

Year End Levels, 1957–60

	1957	*1958*	*1959*	*1960*	*1961*	*1962*	*1963*	*1964*	*1965*	*1966*	*1967*	*1968*
Total held	134.8	151.6	161.5	176.8	197.5	226.2	255.7	286.1	319.2	338.3	379.0	412.1
At commercial banks	57.8	65.8	67.5	73.3	82.7	98.3	112.6	127.2	147.2	159.3	183.1	203.7
Corporate business	1.0	1.9	1.5	2.8	4.6	8.3	12.2	15.4	19.2	18.6	22.7	24.8
State and local government	2.8	3.6	3.2	4.6	5.5	6.5	8.1	9.8	12.2	13.5	15.9	19.1
U.S. government	.3	.3	.3	.3	.3	.3	.3	.3	.3	.2	.3	.4
Mutual savings banks	.1	.2	.1	.1	.2	.2	.1	.2	.2	.2	.2	.3
Foreign	3.1	4.0	3.1	3.5	3.8	4.3	5.3	6.7	7.3	8.2	9.6	9.5
Households	50.5	55.8	59.4	62.2	68.4	78.7	86.6	94.8	108.0	118.7	134.5	149.6
At savings institutions	77.0	85.9	94.0	103.5	114.8	127.9	143.1	159.0	172.0	179.0	195.9	208.4
Liabilities												
Savings-and-loan assns.	41.9	48.0	54.6	62.1	70.9	80.2	91.3	101.9	110.4	114.0	124.5	131.6
Mutual savings banks	31.7	34.0	35.0	36.3	38.3	41.3	44.6	48.8	52.4	55.0	60.1	64.5
Credit unions	3.4	3.9	4.4	5.0	5.6	6.3	7.2	8.2	9.2	10.0	11.2	12.3
Assets												
Households	76.6	85.3	93.5	103.1	114.3	127.3	142.4	158.1	171.3	178.4	195.0	207.8
Credit union deposits at savings and loans	.4	.6	.5	.3	.5	.6	.7	.8	.5	.5	.8	.6
Memo—Households total Time and savings accounts	127.0	141.1	152.8	165.3	182.6	206.0	229.0	252.9	279.3	297.1	329.5	357.4

Source: Board of Governors of the Federal Reserve System, *Flow of Funds Summary*, February, 1970.

TIME DEPOSITS, RESERVES, AND MONEY SUPPLY

Banks are required to hold reserves against time as well as demand deposits, although the required reserve percentages are much lower. Increases in time deposits therefore absorb reserves, reducing the amount of reserves available for demand deposits (unless the Federal Reserve engages in a compensating open-market operation). However, since the reserve requirements for time deposits are in fact much lower than for demand deposits, an increase in time deposits results in a net expansion of bank assets and liabilities, even if total reserves are unchanged.

The T accounts below show the effect of a $1-million increase in time deposits with total reserves unchanged. Suppose a business customer buys a certificate of deposit with a check drawn on his demand deposit account (in the same bank). Initially the bank's total assets and liabilities remain unchanged. The increase in time deposit liabilities has balanced the decrease in demand deposit liabilities. However, if the reserve ratio is 15 per cent on demand deposits and only 5 per cent on time deposits, its required reserves are reduced by $100,000. The bank now has excess reserves worth $100,000. It can buy securities or make loans with the $100,000, just as though it had obtained excess reserves through a Federal Reserve open-market operation. From here on, the expansion process proceeds just as in the example on pp. 29–33. The initial excess reserves will permit the banking system to create $0.67 million of new demand deposits and to acquire $0.67 million of new earning assets. The net change in the consolidated balance sheet of the banking system is shown in the second T account.

COMMERCIAL BANK BALANCE SHEETS

Changes Due to a Shift from Time to Demand Deposits

Initial Effect

Assets	*Liabilities*
Required Reserves — 100,000	Demand Deposits — 1,000,000
Excess Reserves + 100,000	Time Deposits + 1,000,000

Final Effect

Assets	*Liabilities*
Earnings Assets + 667,000	Demand Deposits — 333,000
	Time Deposits + 1,000,000

During the early 1960's, open-market operations provided enough reserves to match the growth of bank time deposits while still permitting a significant expansion in demand deposits. Much of the effect of the expansion in bank time deposits was to divert credit flows from thrift institutions to the commercial banks. However, as we shall see in Chapter 7, it also had significant effects on the level and structure of interest rates.

After 1965, the regulation *Q* ceiling again inhibited the competition for time deposits, and as we shall see in Chapter 7, the *Q* ceiling played a major role in monetary policy.

CYCLICAL MOVEMENTS IN BANK ASSETS

We have noted a number of ways in which banks respond to changes in loan demand and changes in Federal Reserve policy. We can now review those adjustments and tie together the reactions of individual banks with the behavior of the banking system as a whole.

During recession periods the Federal Reserve usually reduces required reserve ratios or buys securities to increase bank reserves. In those periods most banks are gaining reserves. Any banks which owe the Federal Reserve can repay it. Banks with increased reserves or lower required reserves can buy securities or make loans. Since loan demand is usually declining in recessions, banks with excess reserves buy United States or state and local securities. As far as an individual bank is concerned, it is simply a matter of paying for securities with a check on its Federal Reserve account. But since the check will be deposited in some other bank, the reserve balances do not disappear when they are used. A fraction of them is tied up in additional required reserves with each round of the multiple expansion process. The process works out just as in the examples given in the preceding chapter except that (1) some of the reserves provided by the Federal Reserve are used to repay debt to the Federal Reserve, and (2) some small banks are slow about investing funds, so that excess reserves increase in recessions. Deposits and bank assets do not grow as much as our theoretical examples in the preceding chapter would suggest.

During upswings in the business cycle, banks find themselves in a quite different position. The Federal Reserve usually adds slowly or not at all to the reserves of the banking system during a boom. But demand for business and consumer loans usually expands rapidly. The loan departments of banks respond to the demand by making many new loans—creating additional deposits in the process. Since the new deposits are spent quickly, the banks making loans lose deposits almost as fast as they create them. And for every dollar's worth of checks drawn on these new deposits, the lending bank loses a dollar's worth of reserves to some other bank.

The banks which lose reserves in that way draw down excess reserves, use their deposits with correspondent banks, sell securities, or borrow from Federal Reserve Banks. Most of the problem is met by selling securities to individuals or corporations. When a bank sells a security to a nonbank individual or corporation, the bank is paid with a check on the buyer's account. The volume of bank deposits is reduced and so is the volume of required reserves. When banks make loans, they create deposits, and when they sell securities, they destroy deposits.

But banks also meet reserve deficits by borrowing from their Federal Reserve Banks. When they do so, the total reserves of the banking system are expanded. An increase in reserves obtained from borrowing provides the basis for a multiple expansion of deposits just as much as an increase in reserves resulting from an open-market operation. Thus the money supply may expand in the upswing even though the Federal Reserve has taken no action at all—except to lend reserves.

The amount of deposit expansion based on borrowing is limited, because the Federal Reserve Banks discourage member banks from borrowing large amounts and from remaining in debt for long periods. An increased demand for bank loans which accompanies a rise in business activity can be partly accommodated by an expansion in bank assets, supported by the use of excess reserves existing at the start of the boom and by borrowed reserves. Banks can make additional loans by selling securities to the nonbank public But those resources are limited. Banks have relatively small amounts of excess reserves even at the start of a boom, and their ability to borrow reserves from the Federal Reserve Banks is limited. The volume of government securities held by banks is very large. But since interest rates are usually rising and security prices falling, only short-term securities can be sold without loss.

As a boom progresses, many banks find that they have sold out most of their shorter-term government securities. They can make additional loans only by taking capital losses on sales of long-term securities. Banks are willing to take some capital losses but not an unlimited amount. They become reluctant to increase their loans. Most banks feel that they must accommodate their good deposit customers; but they refuse loans to others, lend less than the requested amount, or make the loan for a shorter period. They engage in "credit rationing."

If the regulation *Q* ceilings permit, banks can seek to meet increasing loan demand by raising the rates offered on time deposits. Large commercial banks can raise their rates for negotiable certificates of deposit and induce corporate treasurers to take "CD's" instead of Treasury bills or commercial papers. Such a shift, of course, tends to push up interest rates on Treasury bills and commercial paper. Banks of all sizes can also raise rates offered on consumer time deposits, attracting funds from savings-and-loan associations and mutual savings banks and ultimately gaining funds at the expense of the mortgage market.

In attempting to attract time deposits, banks must recognize that an increase in rates must be paid to a large proportion of depositors, not just to the new ones. The additional interest cost for an additional dollar of deposits (marginal cost) may be far greater than the rate quoted. Furthermore, in the case of consumer-type time deposits, it may take a long time before everyone has reacted to the change in rates. The marginal cost of additional deposits may therefore rise above the yield of assets; moreover, it may check competition for time deposits, if the regulation *Q* ceiling does not do so first.

In a long period of expansion, banks may sell out most of their short-term securities and reach the limits of their ability to compete for time deposits.

Variations in Federal Reserve policy and in business activity affect the availability of credit through the accompanying efforts of thousands of individual banks to adjust their reserve positions and portfolios to changing conditions. When the Federal Reserve supplies banks with additional reserves, banks become eager to expand loans. When reserves are not expanding and loan demand increases, loans become hard to get. Thus part of the varying tension between Federal Reserve policy and business conditions is reflected within the banking system. But since banks sell off securities to make loans, they pass part of the effect of changing conditions on to the rest of the financial markets. We shall consider those other markets in the next chapter.

SUMMARY

Commercial banks engage in a great variety of activities, but their main business consists of accepting deposits and investing in loans and securities.

In making their investment decisions, bank managements naturally wish to invest in the assets that produce the highest net return (after allowance for investment costs and losses). At the same time, however, they must avoid taking any serious chance of loss, which might render the bank insolvent. They must also be prepared to meet deposit withdrawals at any time. They must, therefore, hold a substantial amount of assets that can be readily liquidated. In addition, they must meet legal reserve requirements and hold enough vault cash to accommodate their customers' requests for currency.

When a bank has provided for deposit withdrawals and met legal reserve requirements, it can invest the remainder of its assets in business loans, mortgage loans, installment loans to consumers, or in federal, state and local, or corporate bonds.

Banks generally give priority to loans to business firms which maintain deposits with the bank. Consumer installment loans have proved particularly profitable to many banks. The demand for business and consumer loans varies over the business cycle. When demand for loans expands more rapidly than deposits, banks sell government securities. In the reverse situation—

usually during recessions—banks rebuild their holdings of government securities. Banks also borrow from Federal Reserve Banks during periods when demand for loans is expanding rapidly, repaying during recession periods. As a result, the money supply may expand during a prosperous period even when the Federal Reserve Banks are not making any open-market purchases. During recessions part of the reserves provided by the Federal Reserve System are absorbed when member banks repay their debts to Federal Reserve Banks.

During periods when loan demand is expanding rapidly, some banks cannot sell enough securities or borrow enough to satisfy all their customers' requests for loans. The banks then tighten the terms on which they make loans and refuse additional loan applications.

Capital Markets

CHAPTER FIVE

When Polonius told Hamlet "neither a borrower nor a lender be," he was not only boring, he was wrong. Borrowing and lending are essential to the operation of a growing industrial economy. Millions of households, and thousands of businesses and governments, save more than they invest and so have surplus funds. Those surpluses must be transferred to others who have deficits (i.e., invest more than they save). That transfer function is performed by a set of securities markets together with a variety of financial institutions and specialized firms, for example, securities brokers and dealers. Collectively these markets institutions and firms are called the capital markets. Households, businesses, and governments are in the capital markets, both as borrowers and lenders. At any point, some households are borrowing to buy houses, cars, or durable goods; others are saving for a rainy day (and many do both). Some governments are investing budget surpluses; others are borrowing to finance deficits. Some businesses are borrowing to finance investments beyond their internal saving; others invest some of their earnings in liquid assets or in other businesses. Figure 5–1 gives some idea of the magnitude and volatility of the different types of demand for capital funds.

The capital markets must continually adjust to these changing pressures in order to maintain a balance between the demand and supply for each type of security and in the market as a whole. That adaptation is achieved through changes in interest rates and the responses of lenders and borrowers to them.

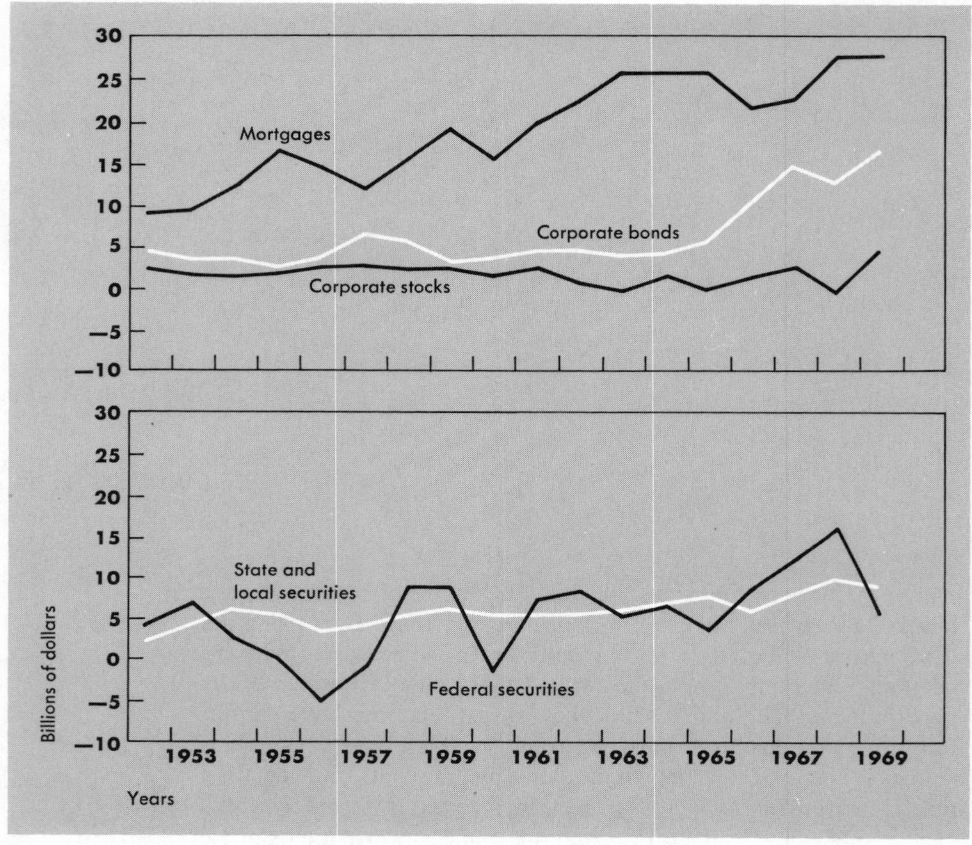

FIG. 5-1 Net new issues of market instruments. (Source: 1952–68, *Flow of Funds;* 1969–70, *Federal Reserve Bulletin.*)

Interest rates influence borrowing and lending in three ways.

1. The level of rates influences the volume of expenditure for business plant and equipment and for residential construction. When businesses invest less, they borrow less. When families buy fewer houses, they borrow less on mortgages.

2. Differences in interest rates on different kinds of securities influence how borrowers obtain their funds and lenders invest their funds. Thus changes in specific interest rates draw money from markets where funds are plentiful to markets where they are scarce.

3. People who save can lend their money or retain it; borrowers can increase their holdings of money by borrowing more than enough to finance

expenditures. Interest rates influence the amount of money people want to hold and thereby the amount they lend or borrow.

SOURCES AND USES OF FUNDS

Corporations

Corporations must finance a continuous expansion in their physical assets: plant, equipment, and inventory. In addition, they must raise funds in order to extend credit to consumers and to unincorporated business customers. Finally, because their receipts and expenditures are uneven and unpredictable, they need to hold large amounts of liquid assets (e.g., demand and time deposits or Treasury bills) in order to meet their obligations in case receipts from operations fall short of expenditures. Liquid asset holdings decline at times, but on the average corporations have to raise funds to keep their liquid asset holdings in line with their growing expenditures.

Corporations meet a large part of their capital needs from internal sources—capital consumption allowances and retained earnings. Indeed, internal sources often equal or exceed physical investment. It is tempting to to say that physical investment is mostly financed from internal sources, whereas financial sources provide for financial uses. But we cannot match particular sources against particular uses. Trade and consumer credit and liquid assets are just as vital a part of business operations as acquisition of physical assets. And some corporations (e.g., public utilities) raise a much greater proportion of their investment funds in the capital markets than others. The principal sources and uses of corporate funds are shown in Table 5–1. It will be noted that in the last few years the excess of investment in physical assets over funds raised from internal sources has increased sharply.

State and Local Governments

Since 1945, state and local governments have raised large amounts in the capital markets every year. Rising income and population have generated strong demands for public capital—highways, schools, water and sewer systems, public housing. Although state and local governments can finance substantial amounts of capital investment from the surplus of tax receipts over current operating expenditures, they have been forced to borrow heavily to meet the demand for public capital. As a result, state and local debt has risen to $130 billion, nearly ten times the amount outstanding at the end of World War II. The average annual increase in state and local debt has risen from $2 billion to $10 billion.

Like corporations, state and local governments have to hold substantial amounts of financial assets. Their tax receipts and expenditures have a marked seasonal pattern so that during part of the year they hold large amounts of

Table 5-1 **SOURCES AND USES OF FUNDS, NONFARM NONFINANCIAL CORPORATE BUSINESS, 1959–69 (Billions of dollars)**

Source or use of funds	*1959*	*1960*	*1961*	*1962*	*1963*	*1964*	*1965*	*1966*	*1967*	*1968*	*1969*
Sources, total	57.9	48.1	56.6	64.9	67.1	71.8	93.1	100.6	94.4	109.8	118.4
Internal sources	35.0	34.4	35.6	41.8	43.9	50.5	56.6	61.2	61.5	62.5	62.5
Undistributed profits	12.6	10.0	10.2	12.4	13.6	18.3	23.1	24.7	21.1	20.9	19.9
Corporate inventory valuation adjustment	—.5	.2	—.1	.3	—.5	—.5	—1.7	—1.8	—1.1	—3.3	—5.4
Capital consumption allowances	22.9	24.2	25.4	29.2	30.8	32.8	35.2	38.2	41.5	44.9	48.0
External sources	22.9	13.7	21.0	23.1	23.2	21.3	36.5	39.4	33.0	47.3	56.0
Stocks	2.2	1.6	2.5	.6	—.3	1.4	.0	1.2	2.3	—.8	4.3
Bonds	3.0	3.5	4.6	4.6	3.9	4.0	5.4	10.2	14.7	12.9	12.1
Mortgages	3.0	2.5	3.9	4.5	4.9	3.6	3.9	4.2	4.5	5.8	4.3
Bank loans n.e.c.	3.5	1.9	.7	3.0	3.7	3.8	10.6	8.4	6.4	9.6	10.9
Other loans	—.3	1.9	.6	.0	.2	.9	.6	1.4	1.4	3.6	6.2
Trade debt	5.5	.6	5.4	4.6	5.3	3.6	9.1	7.3	2.6	5.7	10.9
Profits tax liability	2.4	—2.2	1.4	.6	1.9	.5	2.2	.2	—4.1	3.7	.8
Other liabilities	3.6	4.0	1.7	5.2	3.7	3.5	4.6	6.5	5.2	6.9	6.5
Uses, total	53.1	43.7	52.2	60.0	63.2	64.9	85.8	92.5	85.5	103.5	111.2
Purchases of physical assets	36.9	39.0	36.7	44.0	45.6	52.1	62.8	77.1	72.0	76.9	87.0
Nonresidential fixed investment	31.1	34.9	33.2	37.0	38.6	44.1	52.8	61.6	62.5	67.5	76.9
Residential structures	1.7	1.1	1.9	2.3	2.6	2.1	2.0	1.1	2.3	2.4	2.9
Change in business inventories	4.1	3.0	1.5	4.7	4.3	5.9	7.9	14.4	7.3	7.0	7.2
Increase in financial assets	16.2	4.7	15.6	16.0	17.7	12.8	23.1	15.5	13.5	26.6	24.2
Liquid assets	5.6	—3.2	3.7	3.5	4.7	1.2	1.7	1.9	.0	10.1	2.3
Demand deposits and currency	—1.0	—.5	1.7	—.9	—.8	—2.3	—1.5	.7	—2.2	1.3	.5
Time deposits	—.4	1.3	1.9	3.7	3.9	3.2	3.9	—.7	4.1	2.2	—7.8
U.S. Government securities	6.6	—5.4	—.2	.5	.5	—1.5	—1.6	—1.2	—3.1	1.8	—1.4
Open-market paper	—.2	1.7	.4	.6	.9	1.6	.5	2.0	1.5	4.5	8.7
State and local obligations	.7	—.2	.0	—.3	.2	.2	.5	1.0	—.4	.4	2.3
Consumer credit	.8	.4	.2	.7	1.0	1.3	1.2	1.2	.9	1.7	1.3
Trade credit	7.7	5.3	9.5	8.5	8.1	8.1	15.1	11.3	8.8	14.8	17.3
Other financial assets	2.0	2.2	2.1	3.2	3.9	2.2	5.1	1.0	3.8	.1	3.4
Discrepancy (sources less uses)	4.8	4.3	4.3	5.0	3.8	6.9	7.2	8.0	9.0	6.3	7.2

Source: Board of Governors of the Federal Reserve System.

liquid assets. In addition funds are often raised in advance for construction projects lasting several years and held in liquid form pending expenditure.

Federal Government

The federal government usually turns out to be the world's greatest everything and its financial operations are no exception. Almost every financial institution, and most corporations and governments, hold part of its $300 billion debt. And because federal securities are so widely held and so readily available, a high proportion of the adjustments in financial positions of businesses, governments, and financial institutions is made by purchase or sale of government securities; thus the yields on government securities are the anchor point in the whole structure of interest rates. The Treasury's financial position changes rapidly, swinging, for example, from a $5 billion debt reduction in 1956 to $10 billion of net borrowing in 1959. But even when the budget is nearly in balance, the Treasury must continuously refinance a large volume of maturing securities, and therefore its operations are always a major factor in the capital markets. In an average year the Treasury must refinance more than $100 billion of maturing securities.

The federal government is not only the largest borrower in the capital markets, it is also the largest lender. Agencies such as the Federal Home Loan Bank Board, the Federal National Mortgage Association, the Farm Credit Administration, and so on raise billions of dollars in the capital market and relend them to home builders, savings-and-loan associations, colleges, farmers, and small businesses. Federal lending agencies generally provide capital for purposes designated by Congress as having special social importance. In some cases the loans are made below market rates and contain an explicit subsidy to the borrower. In other cases, the borrowers pay the full cost (interest and administrative expenses of the lending agency) but benefit because the borrower (e.g., a small college) could not borrow as cheaply as the federal government.

Households

Although businesses and governments lend as well as borrow, they are almost always net borrowers. Households borrow as well as lend, but the household sector is always a net lender.

Like businesses, households finance a large volume of physical investment—mainly consumer durables and houses—and borrow large sums to do so. In a single year consumers may borrow as much as $100 billion, most of it being repaid within the year. The net increase in outstanding consumer installment debt has averaged over $8 billion per year in the last five years. The bulk of this huge credit flow is associated with the purchase of automobiles and other consumer durables. The financing of owner-occupied houses has led to the creation of an even larger volume of household debt. Outstanding mortgage debt on one- to four-family houses has reached $275 billion and grows by $10–13 billion per year. The gross flow of mortgage credit on one- to four-family houses amounts to more than $40 billion.

While some consumers are borrowing to buy durables or houses, others are saving still greater amounts. On the average, households have acquired $50 billion per year of financial assets in each of the last five years. This figure includes their net purchases of bonds and stocks and the increase in their holdings of currency, demand deposits, and time deposits. It also includes the increase in their net claims against life insurance companies and pension funds. To these vast sums must be added the increase in the value of common stocks which, although much more volatile than other forms of saving, are almost equally important.

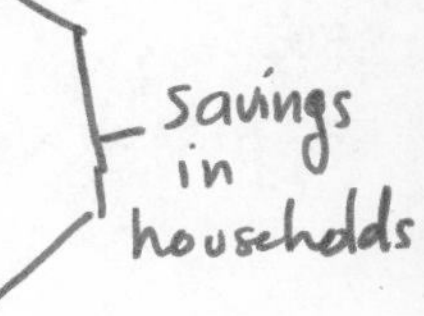

The financial activities of households are summarized in Table 5–2. It will be noted that in most years the bulk of household saving has been invested indirectly through commercial banks, mutual savings banks, savings-and-loan associations, life insurance, and pension funds.

Table 5-2 **SAVING BY INDIVIDUALS, 1960–69 (Billions of dollars)**

	Increase in financial assets							*Net investment in*			*Less: Increase in debt*		
				Securities									
Year	*Total*	*Currency and Demand Deposits*	*Savings Accounts*	*Government Bonds*	*Corporate and Foreign Bonds*	*Corporate Stock*	*Insurance and Pension Reserves*	*Nonfarm Homes*	*Consumer Durables*	*Noncorporate Business Assets*	*Mortgage Debt on Nonfarm Homes*	*Consumer Credit*	*Other Debt*
1960	28.7	—1.9	12.4	2.9	.2	—.4	11.7	14.5	5.1	2.1	10.8	4.6	5.4
1961	31.3	1.3	17.4	.7	.3	.4	12.2	12.0	2.9	3.2	10.9	1.8	8.8
1962	37.3	2.9	23.4	.8	—.6	—2.1	12.8	12.8	6.7	5.6	12.7	5.8	8.5
1963	38.9	5.5	23.0	4.3	—.6	—2.8	13.9	12.6	8.9	6.9	14.8	7.9	11.9
1964	45.2	6.5	23.9	4.2	—.5	.0	15.3	12.5	11.2	6.2	16.0	8.5	11.4
1965	52.5	7.3	26.4	4.4	.7	—1.9	17.2	12.0	14.8	9.0	15.2	10.0	13.9
1966	56.1	3.1	19.1	9.5	2.0	—1.0	18.0	11.5	15.2	7.2	12.3	7.2	12.7
1967	62.7	11.5	32.5	—1.4	4.0	—4.8	20.0	9.2	12.4	8.2	10.5	4.6	18.6
1968	57.3	6.9	27.7	6.9	4.6	—7.7	19.5	13.0	17.0	7.6	4.9	11.1	17.9
1969	55.3	3.4	11.3	16.8	4.9	—4.3	20.3	13.2	17.3	8.8	116.3	9.3	14.7

Source: Board of Governors of the Federal Reserve System.

TYPES OF MARKETS

The process of transferring funds from lenders to borrowers is necessarily a complex one. Funds must be raised from millions of individuals and business firms and passed to business, government, and household borrowers. In the process, the credit standing of borrowers must be investigated and terms of payment and interest rates established. Moreover, there must be facilities for the resale of existing securities. These processes are accomplished by a variety of arrangements collectively called capital markets. These markets are specialized to particular types of securities and can be roughly divided into two categories: (1) primary markets (for new securities) and secondary markets (for trading old securities), and (2) open markets (where buyers and sellers compete with one another directly) and negotiated markets (where borrowers try to arrange terms privately with a single lender with the option to go elsewhere if they think they can do better).

Equity Markets

New issues of common or preferred stocks are ordinarily sold through underwriters (often called investment bankers), who buy the whole issue from the originating corporation and then try to retail the shares to individuals, trustees, pension funds, and mutual funds. Underwriters make a profit by buying from the issuer at a price below the offering price to the public, but they risk being left with unsold shares to dispose of at sacrifice prices.

Once shares have been issued, they may be resold again and again in the secondary stock markets. Shares of relatively large, well-established corporations are listed and traded on the New York and the American Stock Exchanges or on regional exchanges. The shares of thousands of less-well-known companies are traded "over the counter." Brokers accept both offers to sell and bids from buyers, and match them when they can.

Corporate and Municipal Bonds

Many corporate and state and local bond issues are sold through underwriters in the same way as stocks. In the case of state and local or public utility bonds, investment banking firms (in groups or syndicates for large issues) bid against one another for the issue. The firm or syndicate offering the lowest yield gets the issue and then retails it to individuals, banks, and insurance companies. However, a high proportion of corporate bonds is sold directly by the issuer to an insurance company or pension fund. In these "private placements" of bonds, the issuer and buyer can negotiate terms to their mutual satisfaction while avoiding the expenses of registering with the Securities and Exchange Commission (SEC) and underwriting. A good many local government issues, especially short-term ones, are sold directly by the issuing government to a local bank. The volume of activity in secondary markets for bonds is much smaller than for common stocks.

U.S. Treasury Bonds

Treasury bonds are usually sold by public subscription. The Treasury sets the terms and then accepts offers to buy. If, as usually happens, the subscriptions exceed the amount of the issue, each subscriber is allotted bonds in proportion to his subscription. Treasury bills are auctioned.

The secondary market for Treasury securities centers on about 25 "dealers" in government securities. Unlike brokers, who only act as agents, a dealer firm buys and sells securities for its own account. Dealer firms buy securities from banks, corporations, and other institutions which need cash, and sell to others who have surplus funds. Dealers cover their costs and earn a profit from the small spread between their buying and selling prices. Dealers carry an inventory of securities which varies from $2 to $5 billion, financing it by borrowing from banks. When the supply of a particular security exceeds demand, dealers accumulate inventory and adjust their position by lowering the price at which they will buy or sell. Since the volume of trading short-term government securities exceeds the volume of trading in stocks, competition among dealers makes this market a very sensitive indicator of the supply and demand for money.

Negotiated Loan Markets

Some of the most important financial transactions are carried out by direct arrangements between borrowers and lenders without the aid of brokers, dealers, underwriters, or organized exchanges. Commercial banks, of course, make loans to businesses and lend on mortgages to home buyers and commercial developers. Savings-and-loan associations and mutual savings banks make an even larger volume of mortgage loans.

In addition, finance companies and mortgage banks lend directly with funds they themselves have borrowed. Finance companies providing installment credit raise their funds by borrowing from banks and by selling bonds and commercial paper. Mortgage bankers lend to real estate developers, using funds obtained from commercial banks; they usually resell their mortgages within a short time to insurance companies, savings banks, and other long-term lenders.

MARKET INTERACTIONS

A vast quantity of funds flows through the capital markets every year. Total transactions in the capital market exceed *$2.5 trillion* in a single year. This enormous flow of funds results in part from the transfer of funds from households, businesses, and governments with surpluses to those with deficits. But it also reflects the constant readjustment of the portfolios of wealth holders in response to changes in their circumstances and to changes in their views about the prospective value of various securities. In the process, the prices of existing securities are constantly changing.

Valuing Securities

The capital markets provide channels through which funds can be transferred from spending units with surpluses to those with deficits. In capital market transactions, the borrowers give promises to make payments in the future in exchange for money now. A 5 per cent 20-year bond with a principal of $1,000 is a promise to pay $50 per year for 20 years with a final payment of $1,000. Once it has come into existence, the bond can be sold again, and its value may vary with the interest rate and with uncertainty about the issuer's ability to fulfill his commitment.

Present Value

It is generally assumed that interest and principal in U.S. Treasury bonds is absolutely guaranteed, yet their value can fluctuate significantly. For example, in early 1970 Treasury bonds due in 1995 with a principal of $1,000 were selling for only $600. Those bonds carried a 2½ per cent coupon when the current interest rate on new government notes was 6½ per cent.

To value a promise to make payments in the future we must start by realizing that money in the future is worth less than money now, because anyone can lend money at interest now and get back more in the future. Today's value of $1 to be received a year from now is not $1. It is the amount you could invest at the going interest rate to receive $1 a year from now. Suppose the going interest rate is 5 per cent. Every dollar invested now will bring $1.05 in one year. To get $1 a year from now, you need to invest $1/1.05 = $.952. The amount $.952 is called the *present value* of $1 in one year discounted at 5 per cent.

How about $1 two years from now? Every dollar invested now will bring $1.05 at the end of the first year. In the second year you earn interest on the first year's interest, so that at the end of the second year you will have $1.05 × 1.05 = $1.1025. To get $1 at the end of 2 years you need to invest now $1/1.1025 = $.907. You can get the present value of $1 discounted at 5 per cent for any number of years by dividing $1 by $(1.05)^n$, where n is the number of years.

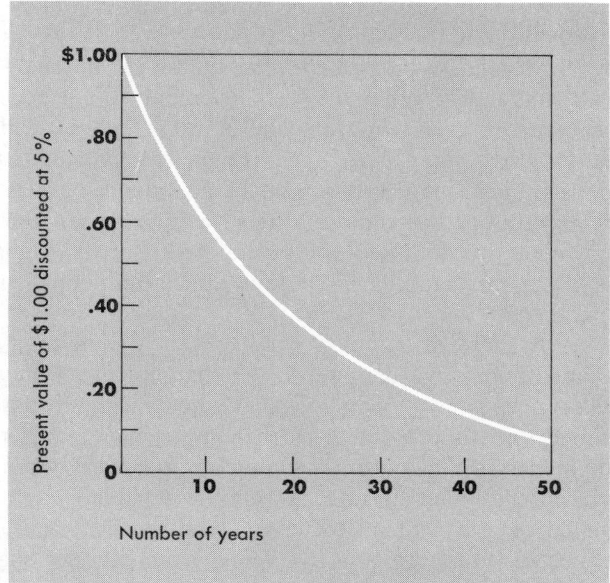

FIG. 5-2 Decline in present value with increase in number of years of discounting.

Figure 5–2 shows how present value declines as the number of years of discounting increases. You can work out the same calculation for any rate of interest. For instance, the present value of a dollar discounted for one year at 8 per cent is only $.926, for two years only $.857. You can see that the higher the interest rate, the less is the present value of money to be received in the future.

To value a bond, we must calculate the sum of the present values of a series of payments for principal and interest. The formula for computing the present value of an investment is

$$V = \frac{y_1}{1+r} + \frac{y_2}{(1+r)^2} + \cdots + \frac{y_n}{(1+r)^n}$$

where V is present value and y_1 is the return in year 1, y_n is the return in year n. The letter r is the interest rate. Notice that a higher interest rate means higher denominators (i.e., greater discounting of the future) and hence lower present value. And the longer the time involved, the greater is the decline in present value caused by a rise in the interest rate.

The effect of changing interest rates on the present value of future payments is shown in the behavior of bond prices. When interest rates rise, all old bonds that were issued when interest rates were low decline in price, but prices of long-term bonds decline much more than those of short-term bonds.

VALUING COMMON STOCKS

No one has ever produced a reliable system for predicting the prices of common stocks. The only safe prediction is one made years ago by J. P. Morgan. When asked what the stock market would do, he replied, "It will fluctuate." The market's movements often seem incomprehensible and the market commentators who always find an explanation for yesterday's events can seldom apply their insight to tomorrow's movements. Yet the underlying logic of the valuation of common stocks is the same as for bonds. In both cases the value of the security rests on the present value of future payments by the issuer to the holders. But the valuation of common stocks is far more complicated because uncertainty and speculation play a much greater part.

A share of common stock is worth something because of the prospect that dividends will be paid to the shareholders. Many stocks are sold at positive prices even though they have never actually paid a dividend—they are worth something as long as there is a chance that they will be able to pay dividends in the future, and they are worthless when everyone becomes convinced that there is no chance of a dividend payment. What is sometimes called the "investment value" of a share of stock is the present value of the expected future stream of dividend payments per share. Thus the investment value of a share of stock that pays a \$1 dividend, and is expected to do so for a long time, is the present value of \$1 per share for an indefinite number of years. Formally the valuation problem is the same as in the case of a perpetual bond (one that pays interest "forever" with no principal payment). The present value of a perpetuity discounted at $d\%$ is $1/d \times \$1$. But in this case the discount rate must be the interest rate on safe bonds plus a substantial risk premium because the dividend is not certain. Thus with a 5 per cent interest rate on safe bonds, the discount factor might be 10 per cent, which would give a value of \$10 per share.

A more common case is that of an average corporation paying out only part of its earnings, investing the rest, and growing at a moderate pace. We might consider a typical corporation earning \$1 per share paying half its earnings in dividends and reinvesting the rest. Suppose that it can be expected to earn an after-tax profit of 10 per cent on reinvested earnings. In a growing economy, that respectable but unspectacular performance could continue indefinitely. Earnings could grow therefore at 5 per cent per year (0.05×0.1) and dividends would grow at the same rate. In that case the stream of dividends to be valued is a growing one at 5 per cent per year. The present value would be $\$0.50\left[\frac{(1.05)}{(1+d)} + \frac{(1.05)^2}{(1+d^2)} + \cdots\right]$.

The same investment value logic can be applied to more complex cases; for example, companies which are expected to grow very rapidly for a limited time and then settle down to a more moderate but continuing rate of growth. Tables are available for valuing securities with a variety of complex growth patterns and with alternative discount rates.

These investment value calculations make sense, and they explain such stock market phenomena as why shares of companies like IBM, with prospects for rapid growth, sell for much higher prices in relation to earnings than shares of companies with more limited growth prospects. And they show how reinvested earnings tend to be reflected in stock prices.

But notice how many assumptions are involved in those "investment value" calculations. No one knows what earnings will actually be next year, let alone how fast they will grow in the future. Yet the investment value calculations are very sensitive to changes in earnings assumptions. Moreover, the discount rates [$(1 + d)$, etc.] can be changed not only by changes in market interest rates but by changes in the discount for uncertainty.

Changes in Stock Values

The factors that enter into the valuation of stocks are not only subjective, they are constantly changing. The earnings prospects for individual companies can be changed in many ways—by development of new products or new processes, by mineral discoveries, by changes in legislation or in the strength of foreign competition, and, of course, by changes in the efficiency of a firm's management relative to its competitors. These changes occur every day. At the same time, all stocks—or large groups of them—can be affected by broader movements. When the public becomes more confident that major depressions can be avoided, the earnings prospects for nearly all stocks are improved and risk discounts are reduced. A rise in interest rates will raise the discount factors applied to prospective dividends. A widespread belief that commodity prices will rise at a more rapid pace is in itself favorable to stock prices, since dollar earnings can grow faster in a world of rising prices. But if the public believes that the inflation will be fought with high interest rates and a tight fiscal policy, or if costs rise faster than prices, the adverse effects on stock values may more than compensate for the favorable ones.

If everyone were interested in long-term investment value and all had exactly the same flow of information for judging the future, the many factors influencing investment value could sway actual stock prices in a corresponding way. In fact, of course, some people become aware of the factors that will change earnings prospects sooner than others. They can buy a stock whose earnings prospects are about to improve at a price based on its old situation. When others become aware of the change, the price rises and the speculator makes a quick capital gain.

Needless to say, the expected improvement in earnings often fails to materialize. The early-bird speculator will get his capital gain, however, if he has correctly guessed that people are going to bid up the price of the stock in expectation of better earnings. From a speculator's point of view, it doesn't matter what actually happens to earnings—only what people think is going to happen. That, of course, opens the way for some speculators to try to guess what other speculators will guess that investors will think. More important, it allows stock prices to develop movements that are, for a time, almost completely detached from the investment judgments discussed earlier. It not infrequently happens that the price of a stock rises rapidly on the basis of some more or less objective factor affecting its future earnings. Once that has happened, speculators may start bidding for the stock merely on the basis of the past price rise. The boom in the stock may then develop momentum and drive the price to a level that could never be justified by the most sanguine estimate of earnings prospects. Usually those bubbles are soon pricked by some unfavorable piece of news which leads speculators to try to sell, and the whole process reverses. Occasionally, as in 1929, that kind of speculative momentum spreads through the whole market with disastrous consequences.

Thus the short-period variations in stock prices reflect a mixture of changes in the objective factors affecting the earnings of corporations and the psychological and speculative forces affecting investors. Over long periods, the value of stocks does move up with the trend of earnings and dividends; but the relation between earnings, dividends, and prices is never easy to predict.

FINANCIAL INVESTMENTS OF HOUSEHOLDS

Every individual saver wants to invest his funds in a way that is consistent with his own needs and plans. People who are primarily concerned with keeping what they have are willing to take a low return on their investments if they can get security of principal. Others are willing to take some risk of loss in return for higher dividend or interest income. Still others are interested in capital gains over long periods and are not much concerned with current income. People in high tax brackets want to get their investment returns in forms that keep down their tax payments. Some people have funds to invest for short periods and want to be able to get their money quickly and easily when they need it. Those who are investing for the long pull do not worry about quick liquidation of their investments.

On the other side of the coin, capital funds are needed by many different kinds of borrowers—by businesses large and small, governments, homebuilders, and people wanting credit for durable goods purchases. Each wants to raise funds in ways that suit his needs. The saver looking for an outlet for his funds finds that there are literally thousands of stocks and bonds and mortgages offering different degrees of safety, liquidity, interest, or dividend returns. Some types of investment (e.g., residential mortgages) require a lot of work in collecting payments, inspecting the property, and seeing that taxes are paid. Others can be made successfully only by someone willing to go to the trouble of investigating the borrower's credit rating. Still others require extensive technical knowledge.

The Pattern of Financial Assets of Households

Corporate stock makes up about half the value of financial assets held by households. The value of common-stock holdings is now eight times as great as at the end of World War II. That enormous increase mainly reflects the change in value of existing stocks in response to increases in corporate earnings and improved confidence in the future. The net value of new corporate stock purchased by households has been relatively small.

Households buy bonds of corporations and governments, along with some mortgages. But aside from United States Savings Bonds, their direct holdings of bonds and mortgages make up a small fraction of their financial assets. The remainder of their assets is in the form of claims against financial institutions—demand and savings deposits at commercial banks, deposits in savings banks, savings-and-loan shares, and claims against pension funds and insurance companies. Some major changes in the financial assets of consumers are shown in Fig. 5–3.

THE GROWTH OF FINANCIAL INSTITUTIONS

The rapid growth of financial institutions reflects some basic changes in the development of the American economy. With the process of industrialization and urbanization, the investment choices facing the public have become more complex, and there has been an increase in the number of families who can save but who do not own a farm or business. Several types of financial institutions have developed to serve the needs of these investors. They include life insurance companies, pension funds, mutual savings banks, savings-and-loan associations, and mutual investment funds, as well as commercial banks. Although many of those institutions, sometimes called financial intermediaries, have existed for a long time, their growth has

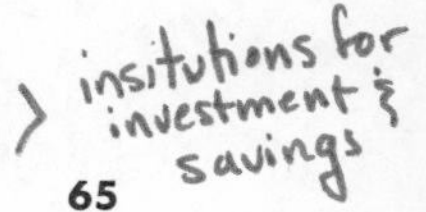

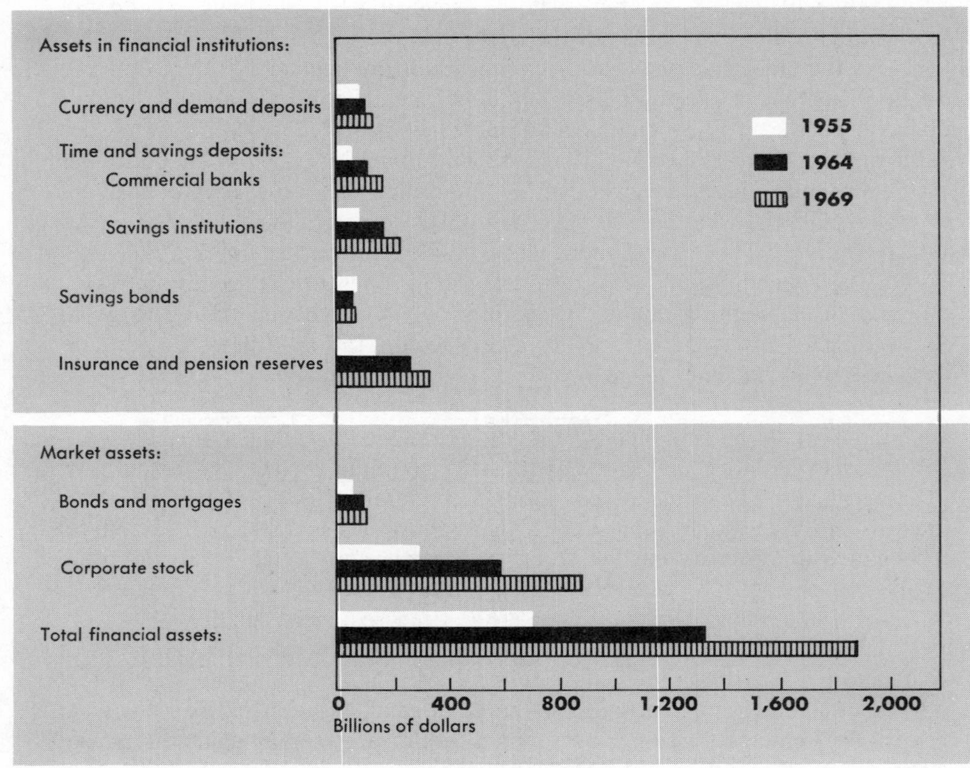

FIG. 5-3 Financial assets of individuals. (Source: *Flow of Funds.*)

been very rapid in recent years. A large proportion of individual savings now flows through these institutions.

Each of these institutions exists to provide some specialized service to investors, but they all help to reduce the risks and cost of investment for individual savers through (1) advantages of scale and (2) diversification.

Advantages of scale. A careful investor must investigate the securities he buys and make comparisons among alternative investment opportunities. This takes time and trouble and may cost money. The job of selecting government securities or stocks costs about the same whether the amount to be invested is a million dollars or a thousand dollars. Moreover, a financial institution investing large sums can afford to hire specialists to investigate and select securities.

In the field of mortgage-lending, financial institutions have a great advantage over individual lenders. Experience with large numbers of loans enables savings-and-loan associations and savings banks to appraise properties and evaluate borrowers' ability to pay much more effectively than any individual lender. This consideration has become increasingly important as the size of cities has grown. A wealthy individual in a small town may know local property and the credit standing of his neighbors as well as anyone. But only a professional can judge the quality of mortgages in Los Angeles. The thrift institutions are also better able to service mortgages. They collect monthly payments, make sure that taxes and insurance are paid, and periodically inspect the properties to see that they are maintained. If the borrower has difficulty making payments, the institution has the staff to make arrangements for refinancing or to take legal action to avoid losses. All these functions can be performed more cheaply on a wholesale basis by a professional staff than by individual lenders.

Diversification. Because of the costs of security selection and purchase, most individuals must limit their investments to a relatively small number of securities. A large financial institution invests in a great many securities. The wisest investor makes mistakes. But when one out of the hundreds of bonds held by an insurance company goes into default, the loss as a percentage of total assets is very small. An individual investor, on the other hand, may lose a significant part of his total holdings when one security goes sour.

All types of financial institutions provide the public with the advantages of large-scale operation and diversification. In addition, each type of financial institution has its own particular function accounting for its growth. Thus life insurance and pension funds provide a family with financial security by providing retirement income and protection against the loss of the family's principal earner. The need for protection of that kind has grown with industrialization, urbanization, and increasing length of life.

THRIFT INSTITUTIONS OFFER LIQUIDITY

Holders of deposits and shares of mutual savings banks and savings-and-loan associations expect to be able to convert their deposits into money at any time. The thrift institutions are able to fulfill that expectation even though most of their assets are invested in mortgages that run for a long period and cannot be readily sold. Thrift institutions hold small amounts of liquid assets—demand deposits and short-term government securities—in case withdrawals should exceed deposits. But thrift institutions have been growing for many years and withdrawals seldom outrun deposits. Thus the holder of a thrift deposit has an asset which he can convert into cash on very short notice, and the institution is able to invest most of its funds in higher-yield, long-term assets.

Financial institutions now play a major role in the process of transferring funds from households with funds to lend to households, businesses, and governments which want to borrow. Because they are professionally managed and alert to small differences in investment returns, they play a major role in the process of allocating loanable funds among competing borrowers.

Competition Among Thrift Institutions

In most areas, households find that a number of commercial banks, savings-and-loan associations, and mutual savings banks are competing for funds. Within the limits permitted by the regulatory authorities, these institutions bid for funds by their interest rate offers; but they also compete by opening new branches, staying open in the evening, and offering various premiums. The thrift institutions are willing to raise interest rates only to the extent that they can invest additional funds at a rate in excess of the rate paid to depositors (and the costs of handling their accounts). Ultimately then, the interest rates offered to households reflect the interest rates determined in the securities markets.

Commercial banks hold a wide variety of assets including a high proportion of short-term securities and business loans, but the investment powers of mutual savings banks are more limited, and savings-and-loan associations are restricted mainly to investments in mortgages and government bonds. Since commercial banks hold many short-term assets, their earnings on these investments rise generally in response to a rise in interest rates. Earnings of savings-and-loan associations, being based on long-term mortgages, rise more slowly. That difference has at times created difficulties for savings-and-loan associations.

Thrift Institutions versus Marketable Bonds

Commercial banks, thrift institutions, insurance companies, and pension funds have attracted the great bulk of household savings in the last quarter century. Unlike the high-tax-bracket investors who buy municipal bonds to avoid income taxes, most households have felt that the advantages offered by the institutions more than outweighed the interest differential required to cover the costs of operating a financial institution. When interest rates rise rapidly, however, the differential between market rates and the rates offered to depositors widens. Financial institutions are not willing to raise deposit rates quickly and then lower them when market rates fall. Moreover, institutions are obliged to raise rates on all deposits, but increased earnings accrue only on *new* funds. Finally, of course, the regulatory authorities have at times used ceiling regulations to prevent increases in deposit rates.

In periods of sharply rising rates (e.g., 1959, 1966, and 1969), market rates have risen relative to deposit rates and some households have shifted funds from deposits to marketable securities—particularly short-term government bonds. Thus in 1965 households bought only five billion dollars worth of government bonds but in 1966 they invested $11 billion in government securities. Those shifts have had significant effects on the lending capacity of banks and thrift institutions.

As the supplies and demands for different types of securities vary, their prices and their corresponding interest rates vary. These variations in turn cause householders to shift their funds between different types of deposits and between deposits and marketable securities. At the same time, changes in interest rates have an important influence on the behavior of businesses and households which are borrowing to make investment expenditures.

INTEREST RATES AND INVESTMENT EXPENDITURES

Business Investment

A growing healthy economy has a large volume of business investment in plant and equipment. In recent years business plant and equipment outlays have amounted to about $100 billion per year.

Managements of business firms are constantly faced with decisions involving investments. They must decide whether to expand capacity or use overtime work to increase output, whether to replace old machinery with new equipment, whether to bring out a new product line or modify an old one. In all these decisions they must weigh the gains from reductions in labor or material costs, or additions to revenue, against the price of the capital goods that produce the cost savings or added revenues. In doing so, they are faced with the fact that they must spend money *now* to earn money *in the future.*

In deciding whether to buy new capital equipment or buildings, managements must first consider whether the cost of the capital goods will be covered by the resulting reduction in labor or material costs or by the value of additional output produced. Since capital goods last a long time, it is necessary to add up the cost savings for each of a number of years and compare the total with the cost of the equipment. Obviously it is never worthwhile to invest unless the total cost savings or extra revenue are enough to cover the cost of the equipment.

But is that enough? If a machine costs $1,000 and saves labor costs by $100 per year for 10 years, would anyone buy it? Of course not. No one wants to trade $1,000 now for $100 each year for 10 years. We all prefer money now to money in the future. If the machine is going to be worth buying, it must produce more than just enough to cover its cost over its lifetime.

A business firm making an investment must compare the capital expenditure involved with the present value of the returns from the investment in future years, and make the investment only if the present value of future returns is greater than the capital outlay required to obtain them. See p. 62 for present value computation. Thus, a firm must estimate the return in each future period, discount it to the present using the interest rate, add up these discounted amounts to get the present value of the future earnings, and compare it with the capital outlay.

An increase in interest rates reduces the present value of the prospective

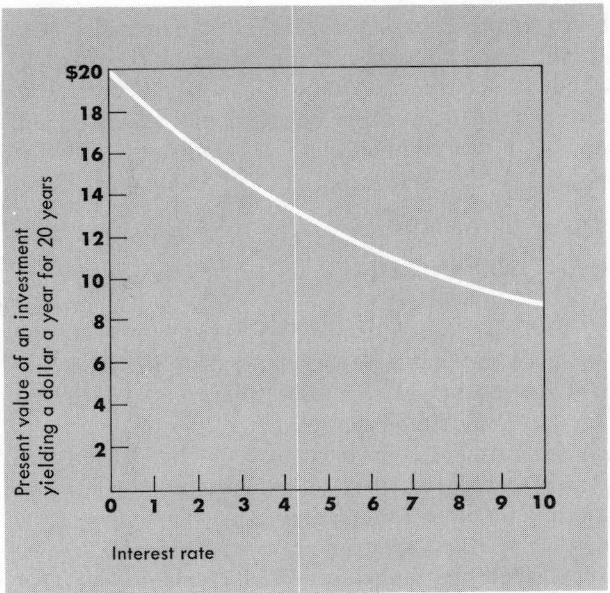

FIG. 5-4 Decline in present value with increase of interest rate.

returns for each future year. Figure 5–4 shows the effect of higher interest rates on a twenty-year investment which earns a dollar a year. You can see how the present value falls with higher interest rates. Suppose the capital outlay for the project is $12. If the interest rate is 5 per cent or less, the project will be worth undertaking. If the interest rate is 6 per cent or more, the cost exceeds the present value and it will not be undertaken. The attractiveness of long-lived projects is very responsive to changes in interest rates. The present value of short-lived projects, such as investment in equipment expected to last only five years, is affected much less by higher interest rates, and spending of this type is less responsive to changes in interest rates.

Every year business firms are faced with thousands of decisions regarding investment. The necessity for making those decisions is an inevitable part of business life in a growing and changing economy in which demand grows and shifts from one kind of product to another, while new equipment and new production methods are constantly being developed. In all problems involving investment, the level of interest rates will influence the final decision. For in all those choices, an investment now will save dollars in the future (or a larger investment will save more future dollars than a smaller one). In making decisions, it is necessary to compare the present value of the dollars to be saved in the future with the investment to be made now. And as we have just seen, projects which would be profitable at a low interest rate will not be profitable at a higher one.

Consider the investment decisions to be made in a particular year. If in that year the interest rate is around 5 per cent, the various choices might result in business decisions to spend $35 billion for the year on plant and equipment. If the interest rate were 6 per cent instead, most of the individual choices would come out the same way. But in a certain number of cases, the difference between a 5 per cent interest rate and a 6 per cent rate would take a project out of the barely worthwhile category and put it in the unprofitable category. So if the interest rate were 6 per cent (all other circumstances the same), the rate of expenditure for plant and equipment might be, say, $33 billion for the year. And if the rate of interest were 4 per cent, some projects that were unprofitable at 5 per cent would become worthwhile; so a 4 per cent rate might be associated with, say, $37 billion of plant and equipment expenditure for the year. Figure 5–5 shows the amount of investment that might be made in a given year, at each of a number of different interest rates.

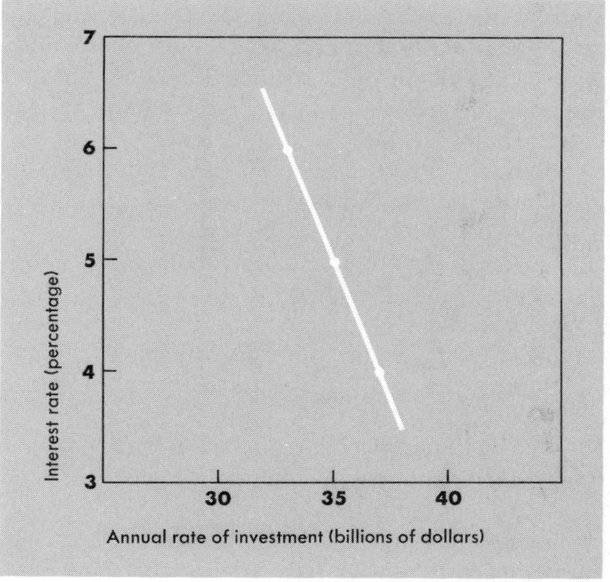

FIG. 5-5 Effect of interest rates on investment.

The examples just given and Fig. 5–5 are hypothetical. Investment varies from year to year for many reasons. It changes with the rate of capacity utilization, with changes in technology, with businessmen's outlook for the future, and for a variety of other factors.[1]

One might suppose that a sufficiently low rate of interest would open up an almost unlimited volume of investment opportunities. After all, there should be an enormous number of projects that would save enough labor

[1] See, in this Series, Charles L. Schultze, *National Income Analysis,* 3rd ed., Chap. 4, for a full discussion.

to cover their cost, given sufficient time. If the interest rate were zero or next to zero, would not all those long-term projects become profitable?

Actually, most of them would not. That money can be lent out at interest is only one reason for regarding a future dollar as worth less than a present one. The future dollars to be earned by buying buildings and equipment are only potential, hypothetical dollars. They may or may not actually be received. A dollar now is a *certain* dollar; a dollar in the future is necessarily an uncertain one. No investment project is guaranteed to yield a return or even recover its cost. The demand for the product of particular buildings and equipment may disappear. The technique embodied in specific equipment may become obsolete any day from tomorrow onward.

Most firms, then, view the future returns from investment with considerable skepticism. Many take the attitude that an investment is not worth making unless it promises to yield enough revenue to cover its costs in, say, five years. And no one is willing to make an investment whose expected return is no greater than obtainable from buying a safe bond.

Moreover, the source of funds used to finance investments makes a difference. As a matter of arithmetic, it does not make any difference whether one pays interest on borrowed money to finance an investment in plant or equipment or foregoes receiving interest by financing it with one's own funds. But a firm runs the risk of getting into financial trouble if it borrows to finance investment projects. The prospective return from an investment project must not only cover interest costs but must be high enough to compensate the firm financing with borrowed money for the extra risk involved.

Furthermore, firms may not be able to borrow all they want, particularly in tight-money periods. Since rising interest rates and credit rationing go together, it is sometimes difficult to distinguish between the effect of interest rates on the demand for credit and the effect of rationing on the availability of credit.

The interest rate is only one of many factors influencing the rate of investment. Variations in interest rate account for only a small part of the total variations in the rate of investment. To determine the net effect of changes in interest rates on investment, elaborate statistical studies are necessary. A number of such studies have been made, but there is still considerable disagreement concerning the change in investment induced by changes in interest rates. The studies suggest that a change in the level of interest rates of 1 per cent (e.g., from 4 to 5 per cent) will change the annual rate of business investment by $1–2 billion. Some economists think the effect may be substantially greater, others think it may be smaller; but all would agree that a change from 5 to 8 per cent would have a significant effect (unless offset by accelerated price increases).

Financing Homes

Home ownership has become a basic element in the pattern of American life. About 60 per cent of American families own their homes, a proportion which has risen rapidly in the past quarter century. Many factors have contributed to this trend, but it would not have been possible without the new arrangements for home financing developed during the depression and immediately after World War II.

Home ownership inevitably requires borrowing. Relatively few families, particularly in the age group in which people wish to acquire their first homes, have enough assets to pay for a house. They have to borrow, and the usual way of borrowing is to mortgage the house being purchased. Most of the home-financing loans are provided by savings-and-loan associations, mutual savings banks, life insurance companies, and commercial banks (especially those with large amounts of savings deposits). Individuals do extend a substantial amount of mortgage credit, but the proportion of mortgages taken by individuals is much smaller now than it was before the Great Depression. A mortgage borrower may deal directly with a local lender, but if he buys a house from a large-scale builder, the builder may arrange the mortgage financing.

Lenders usually require borrowers to make a "down payment" on the house. That is, the lender will lend only a fraction of the purchase price. Until about twenty years ago, lenders typically required down payments of 30 to 40 per cent of the purchase price, but in the last few years, many lenders have been willing to accept down payments of as little as 10 per cent.

Most mortgages today are "amortized." A payment schedule is arranged so that a constant monthly payment covers interest and repayment of the principal over a period ranging from 10 to 30 years. At the outset, most of the monthly payment is required for interest, and only a fraction of the payment is used to reduce the principal of the loan. As the amount outstanding declines, the interest charge becomes smaller and the amount paid on the principal increases. As time passes, the borrower's equity (value of the house less debt) tends to increase. Of course, the required monthly payment increases with the interest rate and decreases as the payment period increases (Table 5–3). You can see from the table that the monthly payment required to buy a house costing a given amount increases as the interest rate increases. Mortgage payments are a substantial part of the total expense of owning a house.

When interest rates rise, potential home buyers have to make a choice between taking less housing or reducing their expenditures on other things. Some will decide not to buy a new home or to buy a less expensive one. Thus an increase in interest rates tends to reduce the rate of residential construction.

Government Insurance and Guarantee

Many people who want to buy a house and can afford large enough monthly payments to carry a mortgage for the full value of the house do not have funds to make a substantial down payment. They are, therefore, unable to obtain ordinary or "conventional" mortgage financing.

In an effort to stimulate home building, the federal government estab-

Table 5-3 **MORTGAGE RATES AND MONTHLY PAYMENTS ON A $20,000, 30-YEAR MORTGAGE**

Mortgage Interest Rate	*Monthly Payments to Principal and Interest*	*Total Monthly Housing Expense **	*Housing Expense as a Per Cent of Typical Family Income ***
5%	$107.37	$195.37	19.8%
5½	113.56	201.56	20.5
6	119.92	207.92	21.1
6½	126.42	214.42	21.8
7	133.07	221.07	22.4
7½	139.85	227.85	23.1
8	146.76	234.76	23.8

* Column 2 plus $88, which is the approximate average amount of other monthly expenses incurred in existing houses financed with a $20,000 FHA mortgage in 1968.

** Based on annual income of $11,825, which is the approximate average (before tax) income of families taking out $20,000 FHA mortgages on existing houses in 1968.

Source: Commission on Mortgage Interest Rates

lished the Federal Housing Administration in the 1930's and authorized FHA to establish a program of mortgage insurance. For a premium of 0.5 per cent of the principal, FHA insures mortgage lenders against loss. Lenders are willing to lend on FHA-insured mortgages with little or no down payment. The Veterans Administration operates a mortgage guarantee program for veterans which is similar to the FHA program.

To protect borrowers from exploitation, Congress then imposed maximum, or "ceiling," interest rates on FHA and VA mortgages. However, the ceilings have not proved effective in lowering interest rates to home buyers. When market rates rise above the ceiling rate, lenders either refuse to lend on FHA and VA mortgages or they obtain an effective interest rate higher than the nominal ceiling rate by "discounting" mortgages. When a lender charges "four points discount" on a mortgage, he pays out only $96 for each $100 of the face amount of the mortgage. Since he will be paid the $100 principal plus interest at the ceiling rate, he earns an effective return on his loan, which is higher than the ceiling rate.

In the tight-money periods of the late 1950's, many institutional lenders were unwilling to charge discounts and simply withdrew from the FHA–VA market. People who did not have funds for a substantial down payment could not obtain conventional mortgages and were therefore unable to buy at all. In the late 1950's the FHA–VA ceilings played a major role in restricting the rate of home building. In recent years the practice of discounting has been more widely accepted, and the ceiling rates have been kept more closely in line with market rates, so that the FHA–VA ceilings have caused less difficulty than in earlier years. But other types of rationing have had an adverse effect on home building.

FLOW OF FUNDS TO THRIFT INSTITUTIONS

Savings-and-loan associations and mutual savings banks have always been the major suppliers of mortgage credit (see Table 5–4). These institutions obtain their funds from household savings and they must compete with commercial banks and with marketable securities to obtain those funds. Generally the thrift institutions are able to hold their own in the competition for funds, but they have difficulties when market rates of interest rise quickly. The year 1966 was a particularly bad one for the thrift institutions. With the expansion of the war in Viet Nam, market rates of interest rose sharply. At the same time, the Federal Reserve Board raised the ceiling rate on commercial bank time deposits. Banks, faced with a strong demand for loans, quickly raised their rates. Notwithstanding the rise in mortgage rates, however, the thrift institutions were unable to raise their rates to depositors enough to meet this competition, since their current revenues came from old mortgages at lower rates. The flow of funds into the thrift institutions dropped sharply as households bought government securities or shifted funds to commercial banks. The thrift institutions in turn had to curtail sharply their mortgage lending.

Table 5-4 MORTGAGE DEBT OUTSTANDING, BY LENDER, 1960–70

(Billions of dollars)

		Selected Financial Institutions					*Other Lenders*	
End of Year	*Total*	*Total*	*Savings-and-Loan Associations*	*Mutual Savings Banks*	*Commercial Banks **	*Life Insurance Companies*	*U.S. Agencies ***	*Individuals and Others*
1960	206.8	157.6	60.1	26.9	28.8	41.8	11.2	38.0
1961	226.2	172.6	68.8	29.1	30.4	44.2	11.8	41.8
1962	248.6	192.5	78.8	32.3	34.5	46.9	12.2	44.0
1963	274.3	217.1	90.9	36.2	39.4	50.5	11.2	45.9
1964	300.1	241.0	101.3	40.6	44.0	55.2	11.4	47.7
1965	325.8	264.6	110.3	44.6	49.7	60.0	12.4	48.7
1966	347.4	280.8	114.4	47.3	54.4	64.6	15.8	50.9
1967	370.2	298.8	121.8	50.5	59.0	67.5	18.4	53.0
1968	397.5	319.9	130.8	53.5	65.7	70.0	21.7	55.8
1969	425.3	339.1	140.2	56.1	70.7	72.0	26.8	59.4
1970	450.0	355.2	149.9	58.0	72.9	74.3	32.1	62.7

* Includes loans held by nondeposit trust companies, but not bank trust departments.

** Includes former FNMA and new GNMA, as well as FHA, VA, PHA, Farmers' Home Administration and in earlier years RFC, HOLC, and FFMC. Also includes U.S.-sponsored agencies such as new FNMA and Federal Land Banks. Other U.S. agencies (amounts small or current separate data not readily available) included with "individuals and others."

Source: Board of Governors of the Federal Reserve System, based on data from various government and private organizations.

Since 1966, the rates on consumer deposits at all institutions have been restricted by regulations so that the thrift institutions were not adversely affected by commercial bank competition when interest rates rose sharply in 1969. However, they did again suffer when savers bought high-yielding government securities.

GOVERNMENT AGENCIES IN THE MORTGAGE MARKET

The difficulties of the mortgage market have stimulated a series of governmental actions to increase the availability of mortgage credit. The basic principle in almost every case is to find a way to channel funds from the bond market into the mortgage market. The Federal National Mortgage Association (Fannie Mae) sells bonds and buys FHA–VA mortgages. The Federal Home Loan Banks also sell bonds to the public. The proceeds from bond sales are lent to savings-and-loan associations, which in turn make mortgage loans. During 1969 FNMA purchased $4 billion worth of mortgages and FHLB's lent $4 billion to savings-and-loan associations. Together they supplied 30 per cent of total mortgage credit during 1969. Housing starts declined during 1969 but they did not fall nearly as far as in 1966, even though interest rates were rising more rapidly than in the earlier year. Many observers feel that FNMA and FHLB operations prevented a disastrous decline in home building. Meanwhile Congress has authorized several other arrangements to channel funds into the mortgage market. Under the new arrangements it should be possible for credit-worthy borrowers to obtain mortgage credit at any time, *provided they are prepared to pay the going mortgage interest rate.* However, home building may still be severely restricted during tight-money periods when the competition of potential home buyers with other investors drives up interest rates.

COMPETITION FOR FUNDS AND THE ALLOCATION OF CAPITAL

All the major borrowers in the capital market—businesses, the federal government, state and local governments, house builders, and consumers—compete for the available funds. That competition is most visible in the case of publicly issued bonds. Securities of the federal, state, and local governments and of corporations are actively traded on highly organized markets. Any issuer of a new security must offer an interest rate which makes a sufficient number of buyers want that security rather than any of the others they could buy.

But borrowers compete with one another even when there is no active market for their securities. There is no regular market for mortgages. But insurance companies and savings and commercial banks will not lend on mortgages unless they can charge an interest rate that compares favorably with the return they could get if they bought bonds instead.

There are other forms of competition. Savings banks and savings-and-loan associations invest heavily in mortgages. A rise in bond yields induces people to buy bonds instead of making deposits at thrift institutions. Indirectly, this draws funds away from the mortgage market. Mortgage rates must be high enough to enable the thrift institutions to compete effectively for savings.

There is also competition among different kinds of securities through choices made by borrowers. Large business firms and finance companies may borrow by selling bonds or by borrowing from banks. The competition among different types of securities is sufficiently intense to make most interest rates move together. See Fig. 5–6. There are differences in the levels of rates be-

FIG. 5-6 Selected interest rates.

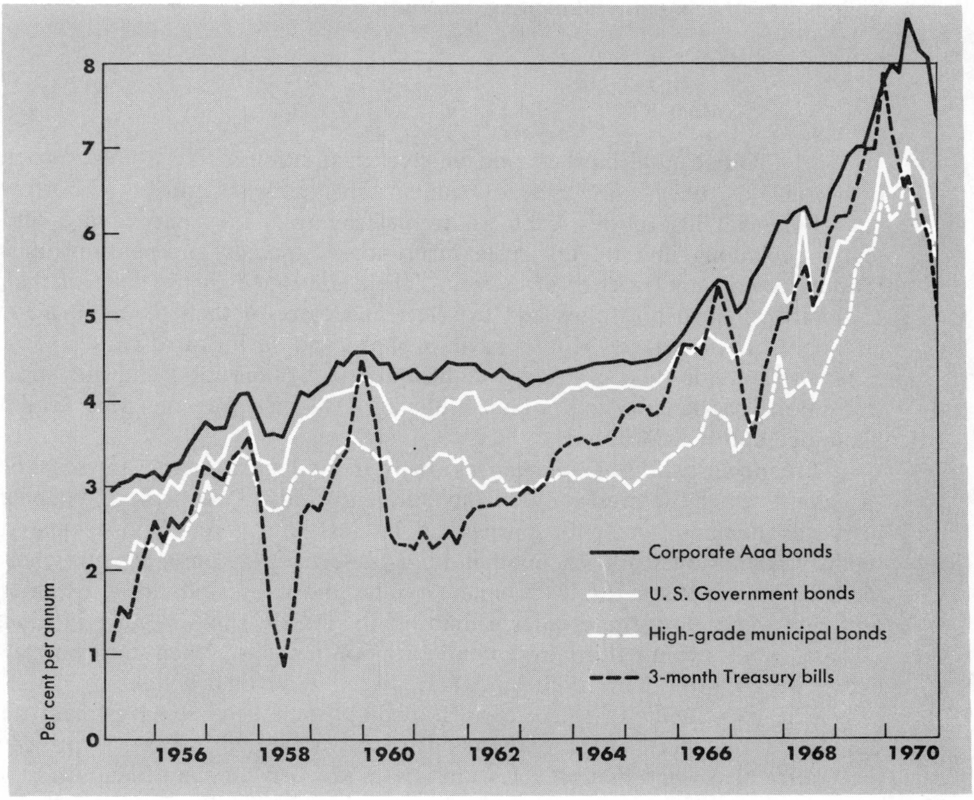

cause securities differ in terms of risk and length of time to maturity, because some have special tax advantages, and for many other reasons. But the interest rates on different kinds of securities do move together. Some move more readily than others. And there are persistent though diminishing geographical differences in mortgage rates and bank lending rates, differences which serve to attract capital from regions where savings outrun investment (such as New England) to regions with particularly strong investment needs (such as the West Coast).

Our capital markets are by no means perfect, but capital funds generally do go to those who are willing to pay the most for them. That is the essential requirement for an efficient allocation of capital resources among competing users. Competition among borrowers and lenders ensures (subject to some qualifications) that any given total of available capital funds will be distributed among potential borrowers in a reasonably efficient way. Those who are willing to pay the most for funds will get them; others will have to do without. And presumably, those who are willing to pay most have the highest return opportunities. Thus the capital market tends to channel the nation's savings into the best investment opportunities.

SUMMARY

Our capital markets and financial institutions serve a great variety of households, businesses, and governments that seek to lend or to borrow.

Financial institutions, such as mutual savings banks and savings-and-loan associations, investments trusts, insurance companies, and pension funds, reduce the cost and risks of investment. Their size makes it possible for them to hold diversified portfolios and to select and care for their assets at a low cost per dollar invested. Mutual savings banks and savings-and-loan associations also provide their customers with liquidity. Urbanization and industrialization and the lengthening human life span have increased the need for life insurance and pension funds.

Financial institutions as well as many individual investors are sensitive to changes in the interest yields from different kinds of securities. When an increased demand for funds pushes up interest rates on any one type of security, some investors sell another kind of security to buy the one whose yield has risen. As a result, all interest rates move up and down together, although some move more quickly than others. And we may regard all kinds of borrowers as competitors for a common pool of funds. When most borrowers are seeking to obtain more funds, all interest rates tend to rise.

The movements of interest rates are important because investment decisions are influenced by interest rates. Business firms find investment projects more attractive when interest rates are low than when they are high. And the cost of owning a house is reduced when interest rates fall. Everyone agrees that changes in interest rates influence the rate of residential construction and the rate of business investment in fixed plant and equipment. But there is a good deal of controversy over the size of the effect of a change in interest rates on business investment expenditures.

Supply and Demand for Money and the Level of Interest Rates

CHAPTER SIX

We have described how funds are drawn from one sector of the capital market to another by relatively slight changes in the differences between interest rates. Let us now turn our attention to the determination of the level of interest rates and to the effect of the level of interest rates on investment and on the economy as a whole.

Differences in interest rates reflect the competition between one kind of security and another kind. From the standpoint of the investor, securities not only compete with one another, but also with money.

Any investor always has the option of holding money instead of other kinds of assets. Savers may use their funds to buy securities or to invest in claims against financial institutions. But they may also simply build up their holdings of demand deposits or currency. People who are not doing any saving may have the option of selling some of their financial assets and adding to their holdings of money.

Business firms borrow to finance investment. But they can, if they wish, sell extra securities to add to their holdings of money. And, of course, if businesses or households want to reduce their money holdings, they are free to act in the opposite way.

The price for holding money rather than securities is the interest which is foregone. For example, if a business wishes to have a cash balance of $1,000 which it may need for payments of its bills, and if the going interest rate on securities is 5 per cent, then the business will pay $50 a year to hold this cash balance.

Thus, money must yield a service which has a value as high as the price being paid to hold it, a value equal to the interest rate.

The level of interest rates must be precisely high enough to induce households and businesses to hold all the money in existence. If interest rates are too low, households and businesses will sell securities or reduce the demand for securities in an attempt to add to their money holdings. This will drive up interest rates. People who most want additional money will get it, while those who least want money will switch to securities in return for higher interest earnings.

In effect, then, the interest rate must be at a level which equates the supply and demand for money. We have already studied how the Federal Reserve determines the supply of money. Let us now consider what determines the demand for money.

HOUSEHOLD DEMAND FOR MONEY

There are three general motives for holding money: (1) the transactions motive, (2) the precautionary motive, and (3) the speculative, or portfolio balance, motive.

Transaction Motive

Everyone wants to have some funds in a conveniently available form, because the time pattern of income receipts does not match the time pattern of expenditures. People may receive most of their income in monthly payments and spend a considerable part of it within the month. They will obviously hold most of the unspent balance in demand deposits or currency.

Some income may be received quarterly or annually and some expenditures (e.g., insurance and tax payments and vacation expenditures) may be on an annual cycle. Funds from large infrequent receipts and for large infrequent payments may be held either in demand deposits or in some form of savings deposits or shares. Such receipts and payments rise as incomes rise. Thus the household demand for money and "near money" tends to rise with the level of personal income.

Money may also be "tied up" in the process of trading assets. People are constantly buying and selling common stocks and other assets. When one man sells a stock to another, the seller receives money which he is likely to hold for some time before he decides how to reinvest it. He may hold a demand deposit until he makes his decision or he may acquire a savings deposit to earn some interest in the interim. Thus the demand for money and "near money" is likely to rise with the amount of transferable wealth.

Precautionary, or Contingency, Motive

Life is full of the unpredictable. Cars break down, houses need major repairs, illness strikes. These things cost money. Many people have to borrow to meet such unexpected expenditures. But most people who have substantial assets like to have funds readily available to meet such contingencies. They could hold all their assets in stocks and bonds and either sell them or borrow against them when the need arises. But most people are willing to give up some interest and hold a demand deposit or a savings deposit to enjoy the feeling of security that comes from having funds immediately available.

Portfolio Balance, or Speculative, Motive

The great bulk of American families never succeed in acquiring more than a few thousand dollars of financial assets. They are likely to hold them in money or near-money form. Most of those families find that the time and trouble and risk involved in buying stocks and bonds outweigh any gains in income they might obtain.

People of wealth generally invest in higher-return assets, but they also hold substantial amounts of money and savings deposits. The rich need contingency reserves like anyone else. In addition, they may be "balancing off" risky investments by holding part of their assets in a safe form.

At any one moment there are some wealthy individuals who want to hold most of their wealth in the form of cash or something close to it. They may believe that securities prices are going to fall or they may feel so uncertain about the future of securities prices that they take a "wait and see" position by holding cash. The force of the "speculative motive" for holding money or near money varies greatly over time. Ordinarily, the amount of money held for speculative reasons is small. But in times of uncertainty or panic, large numbers of people may try to get out of securities and into cash, in the expectation that security prices will fall and that interest rate yields will rise.

DEMAND FOR MONEY AND LIQUID ASSETS RELATIVE TO INCOME

As income rises, the amounts of money households want to hold for all these purposes tend to increase. Transaction requirements tend to rise in rough proportion to the volume of transactions. The amount that is needed to cover the risk of illness, unemployment, and other contingencies increases with the standard of living. And, of course, the aggregate amounts needed for those purposes increase with the growth of population.

The amount of liquid assets required for asset management is not directly connected with income but with wealth. But it is certainly true that wealth grows with income. Thus there is a general tendency for the demand for liquid assets to grow in proportion to income. But many other factors also influence the need for liquid assets. Transaction requirements may change with changes in payment methods. People who are paid weekly will hold less money on the average than those who are paid monthly. The use of credit cards, charge accounts, and installment credit may reduce cash holdings. Unemployment insurance and health insurance and the availability of installment credit reduces the need to save for emergencies. On the other hand, people are able to set aside more for such contingencies as their incomes rise.

Finally, the amount of liquid assets people want to hold varies with confidence about the future. People who worry about unemployment or business losses certainly will hold more cash than people who expect steadily rising incomes.

COMPETITION BETWEEN MONEY AND OTHER LIQUID ASSETS

For many purposes, "near monies" are as good as money. Savings deposits, savings-and-loan shares, or United States Savings Bonds are forms of wealth which have a guaranteed dollar value and are relatively liquid.

But demand deposits are more convenient than any of the others. You can write a check against a demand deposit. You cannot spend any of the other assets without first converting them into money—e.g., by presenting your passbook at a savings bank, getting a check from the savings bank, depositing the check with your commercial bank, and *then* writing a check.

On the other hand, you do not receive interest on demand deposits as you do on the other forms of liquid assets. It costs something to have the greater convenience of demand deposits. The "price" of holding demand deposits is the amount of interest lost by not using one of the other forms of liquid assets.

Obviously, the significance of the convenience of demand deposits and the income from other forms of liquid assets varies with the purpose for which the assets are being held. If your only liquid asset is the unspent portion of the pay check you received on the first of the month, there is not much point in keeping it in a savings account. You would have to go to a lot of trouble to make withdrawals every time you want to pay a bill or get some currency. And you would not receive much interest, if any. On the other hand, a man who has saved $5,000 for a "rainy day" is in a different position. He can earn $50 a year even if the savings deposit rate is only 1 per cent. And he earns it with very little trouble because, hopefully, "rainy days" won't come very often. In between there are people who hold varying sums in liquid form for varying lengths of time. We generally expect that people who hold large sums in liquid form for long periods of time will hold them in a form which yields interest. Small sums held for short periods will be held in demand deposits and currency.

But as the interest rate on savings deposits rises, we expect the proportion of liquid assets held in money form to decline. At a 1 per cent interest rate, a person earns $50 on a $5,000 deposit. At 4 per cent, $1,250 will earn

$50 a year, as will $5,000 held for 3 months. As interest rates rise, then, we expect savings deposits to attract funds held for short periods or in smaller amounts and therefore to attract a greater share of the total.

(During the late 1930's the interest rates offered by thrift institutions were very low and the share of currency and demand deposits in the total liquid assets of households reached 35 per cent. Since the end of World War II, the share of currency and demand deposits in total liquid assets of households has fallen almost continuously. It is now below 20 per cent. Only a part of the change can be attributed to interest rates, but there seems to be little doubt that the post-war rise in interest rates has induced households to hold less money in relation to their income and wealth.)

BUSINESS DEMAND FOR MONEY AND LIQUID ASSETS

Businesses hold large amounts of money and liquid assets and for the same general reasons as do households. Businesses need funds for ordinary, day-by-day transactions because their receipts and expenditures are differently timed. During certain parts of the month or certain seasons of the year, they receive more than they pay out, and at other times they pay out more than they receive. Business firms take care of variations in receipts and expenditures by borrowing at some times of the year and repaying at others. But unless the treasurer wants to borrow or repay every few days, he needs a substantial cash balance for operating purposes.

Businesses also hold liquid assets for precautionary purposes. Every business wants to be able to survive a slack period without having to sell long-term assets or having to borrow on unfavorable terms, and certainly without going bankrupt. And every business wants to be able to take advantage quickly of favorable investment opportunities.

Finally, businesses have a speculative motive for holding liquid assets. When interest rates appear abnormally low, corporate treasurers may borrow and build up liquid assets. They expect to use those funds later when interest rates are higher.

Businesses also have a choice between holding money and other liquid assets. They may hold money or they may hold Treasury bills or time deposits. Like households, they will switch from cash into other liquid assets when interest rates rise enough to make it worth the cost and inconvenience.

SUPPLY AND DEMAND FOR MONEY AND THE LEVEL OF INTEREST RATES

At any given level of income and wealth, households and businesses will want to hold a certain amount of liquid assets. As interest rates rise, a progressively greater share of household liquid assets will be held in the form of savings deposits, savings bonds, or savings-and-loan shares. And as interest rates rise, businesses will tend to hold a higher proportion of their liquid assets in the form of treasury bills or time deposits and a smaller proportion in the form of cash.

Liquidity Preference—The Demand Curve for Money

The demand curve for money looks like any other demand curve, with the interest rate as the price of money (see Fig. 6-1). Households and businesses want to hold more money when interest rates are low. They are willing to buy more "liquidity" when it is cheap. This particular demand curve has been given the name, "liquidity preference schedule."

The curve in Fig. 6-1 is drawn for a given level of income and wealth. We have already mentioned that, at a given interest rate, the need for money increases as income and wealth increase: people need more money for ordinary day-to-day transactions and contingencies, and more money is allocated to buying and selling assets. Not one schedule, but a whole series, one for each level of income and wealth, relates the interest rate and the demand for money.

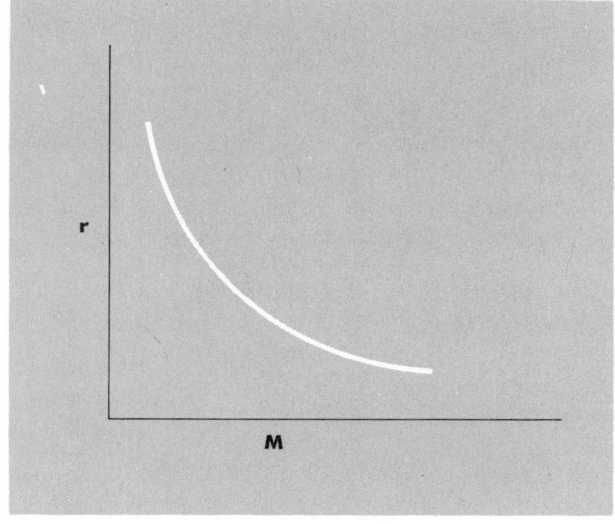

FIG. 6-1 Liquidity preference: Demand for money related to interest rates.

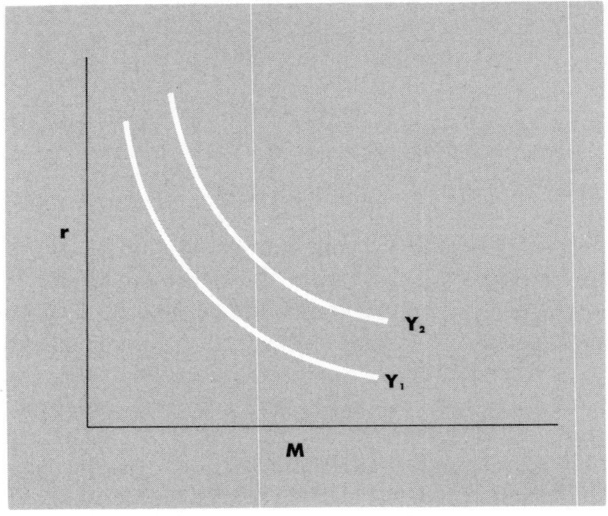

FIG. 6-2 Demand for money related to interest rates and income.

In Fig. 6-2 the curve marked Y_1 represents the demand for money at one level of income; Y_2 is the demand for money at a higher income.

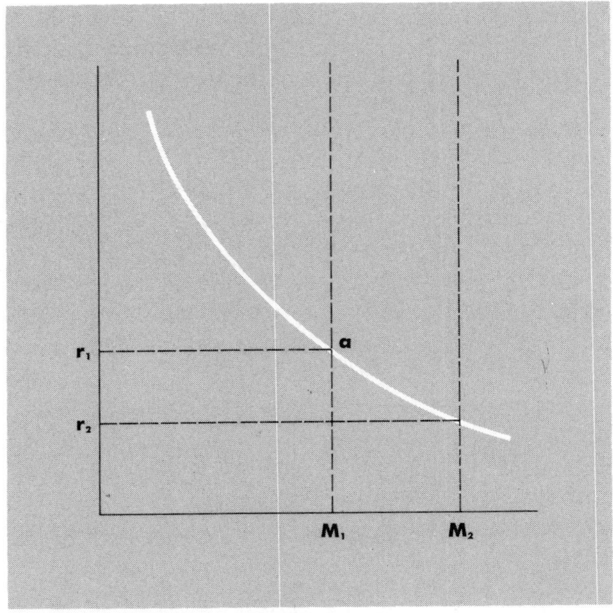

FIG. 6-3 Effect of change in money supply on interest rate.

Determining the Interest Rate

We can regard the supply of money as being determined by the Federal Reserve System. Since it is independent of the interest rate, we represent it as a vertical line in Fig. 6-3.

At any given level of income and with any given supply of money, the interest rate is set at the intersection of the supply and demand for money. In Fig. 6-3 the money supply is M_1. At the interest rate r_1, people are just willing to hold that amount of money.

Effect of a Change in Money Supply

If the Federal Reserve should increase the supply of money, the supply curve would shift to the right and supply and demand for money would be equated at a lower level of interest rates. Thus in Fig. 6-3 an increase in the money supply from M_1 to M_2 reduces the interest rate from r_1 to r_2.

The Effect of a Change in Income

Suppose, on the other hand, that the level of income were to rise while the supply of money remained constant. Then the whole demand schedule for money would shift upward to the right. Supply and demand for money would be equated at a higher level of interest rates.

In Fig. 6-4 the money supply is M_1. The demand for money is shown by the curve marked Y_1. The equilibrium interest rate is determined by the

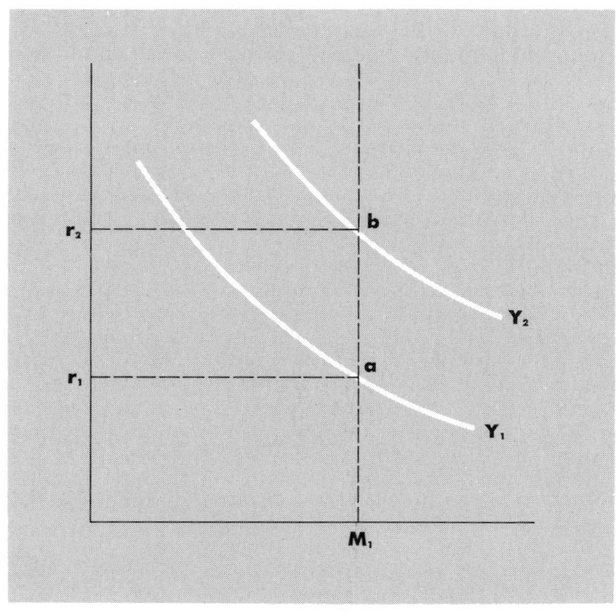

FIG. 6-4 Effect of change in income on interest rate.

intersection of the vertical line M_1 with the curve marked Y_1 at point *a*. The interest rate is r_1. An increase in income increases the demand for money at every interest rate. The new demand-for-money curve is Y_2. It intersects M_1 at point *b*, so the new equilibrium interest rate is r_2.

Adjustments of Interest Rate to Income Change

If expenditures and income are to rise without an increase in the money supply, then businesses and households must be induced to remain content with a constant volume of money even though the value of transactions has increased. A higher rate of expenditure means more employment at higher wages and consequently more money in people's pockets, and more money held in bank accounts between the receipt of wages and their expenditure. Businesses too will have more in their cash registers and will be piling up larger bank balances in preparation for the payment of wages and other bills. And, if the higher level of income persists for a time, people will wish to hold more liquid funds for contingency purposes. At the same time, the value of assets will rise and the amounts of money tied up in the purchase and sale of assets will tend to increase.

Something has to give. Households that want more cash can get it by not lending all their savings. Businesses that want more can get it by borrowing more than they need to finance investment. *But not all of them can increase their holdings of money simultaneously.* Competition for the limited supply of funds—in the form of efforts to borrow or refusals to lend—will drive up interest rates. Those who find it least inconvenient to get along with less money will be willing to earn (or avoid paying) the higher interest instead. Thus those who need to increase their cash position most and who are willing to pay for the privilege will get more of the limited supply of money available.

FIG. 6-5 Left, demand for money; right, relation between investment and interest rate.

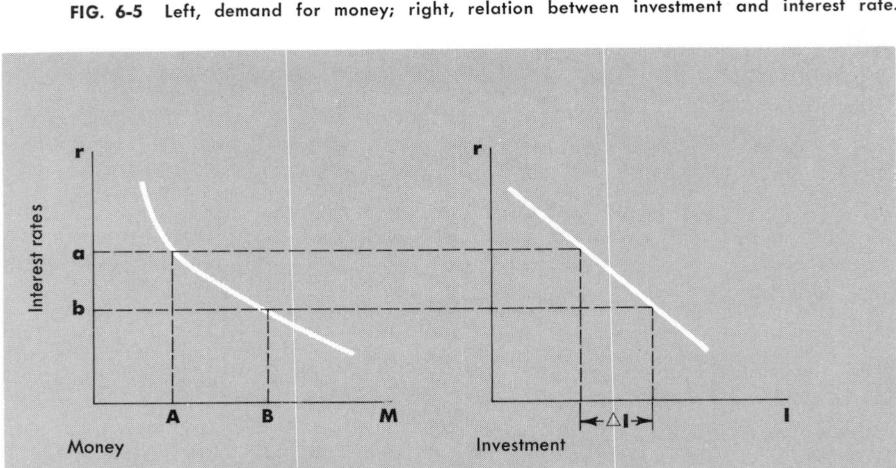

The interest rate is the price of holding money, and it responds like any other price. An increase in expenditure increases the demand for money —shifts the demand curve to the right. If the supply of money is fixed, the price (interest) rises. As the economy grows, it needs additional money. Otherwise the interest rate is driven higher and higher, slowing down growth.

MONEY SUPPLY AND NATIONAL INCOME

The Federal Reserve controls the money supply, the money supply influences interest rates, and interest rates influence investment. By increasing or decreasing the money supply, the Federal Reserve can influence the rate of investment. And the rate of investment is an important determinant of the level of income. Using the theory of national income analysis let us examine this process in detail. Figure 6-5 shows both the demand for money and the relation between investment and the interest rate (sometimes called the marginal efficiency of investment schedule). When the Federal Reserve increases the money supply from A to B, the interest rate will fall from a to b according to the demand for money curve. With a lower interest rate, investment will increase by ΔI.

how FRB can change investment

But the increase in investment is not the end of the story. The multiplier has to be applied to this increase. Figure 6-6 shows how the increased investment leads to a higher GNP. Line CC reflects the consumption function. $C + G + I$ is the total spending line for any given Gross National Income. Point c is the initial equilibrium point, where GNP = GNI. With investment increased by ΔI, GNP will move up to d. Thus, an increase of the money supply has produced a decline in the interest rate, which resulted in an increase in investment, which through the multiplier has led to an additional rise in GNP.

The effectiveness of monetary policy depends on the shapes of the curves in the diagrams. During the depression, many economists became pessimistic about the stimulating power of easier money. Figure 6-7 summarizes this view. Even a large increase in the money supply produces only a small decline in the interest rate. Because of the speculative motive—the fear that security prices will fall—people hang on to their cash rather than invest it. More money is absorbed by people's great preference for liquidity. And the demand for investment is unresponsive to cheaper and more abundant credit in a depression. When things look really poor, investment may remain low even as the interest rate approaches zero.[1]

[1] Not all scholars share this view. Professor Milton Friedman, in his *A Monetary History of the United States,* argues that in deep depression a vigorously expansionary monetary policy, raising M even as the economy contracts, could turn the tide and produce expansion.

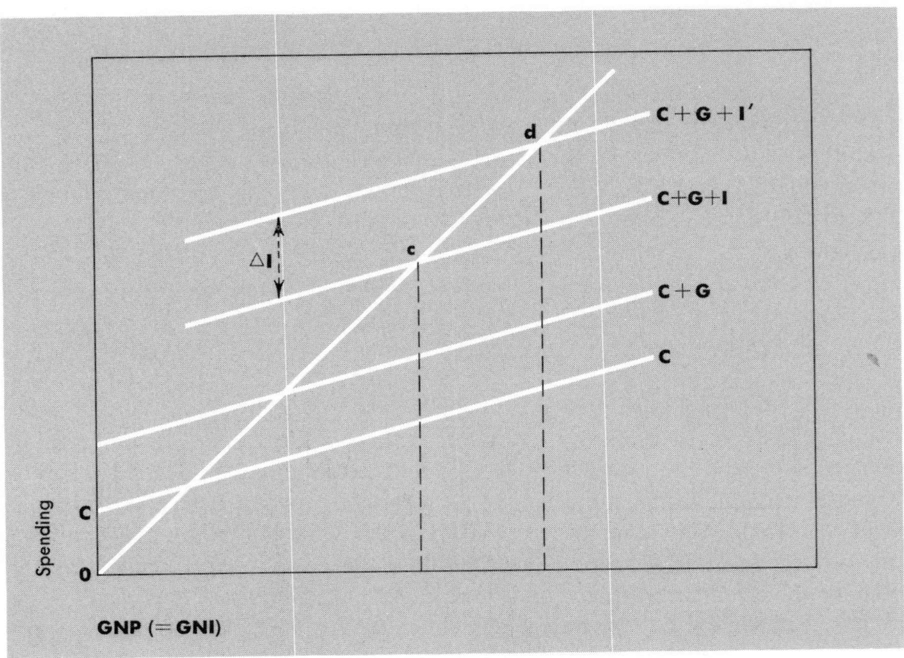

FIG. 6-6 Determination of equilibrium level of GNP.

In more normal times, the reactions to a bigger money supply are more likely to correspond to Fig. 6-6. But there is still considerable disagreement among the experts about the exact pattern of response—i.e., about the shapes of these curves; and the response will of course be affected by various other circumstances at any particular point in time.

MONETARY POLICY AND FULL EMPLOYMENT

Full employment is one of the major goals of economic policy. To achieve it, total spending must equal potential GNP at the target level of unemployment. In Fig. 6-8 the level of gross national product marked *FE* corresponds to a target rate of unemployment. That rate will be achieved if the $C + I + G$ line crosses the 45° line at point *a* over point *FE*. The line $C' + I' + G'$ yields an equilibrium level of income lower than *FE* and results in too much unemployment. The line $C'' + I'' + G''$ produces an equilibrium level of income to the right of *FE*. There is too much demand and consequently inflation.

Notice that what counts is the *total* of consumption plus government expenditures plus private investment expenditures. If the total is too high

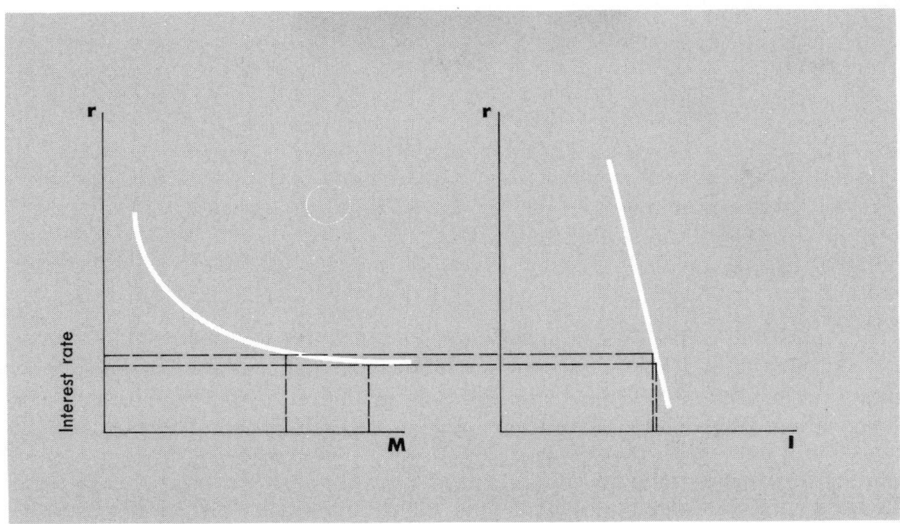

FIG. 6-7 Depression view of monetary policy.

or too low, policy measures are available which will raise or lower any one of the three components.

Taxes can be raised or lowered to raise or lower consumption, and government expenditures can be raised or lowered directly. The money supply can be increased to raise *I*, or reduced to lower it. Other measures such as changes in business taxes can also be used to raise or lower *I*.

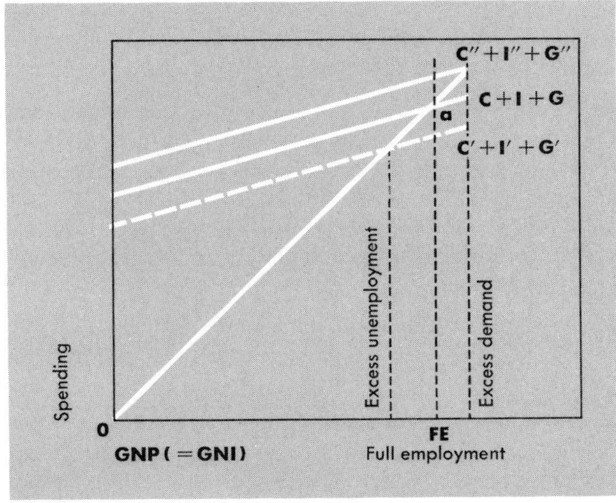

FIG. 6-8 Total spending required for full employment.

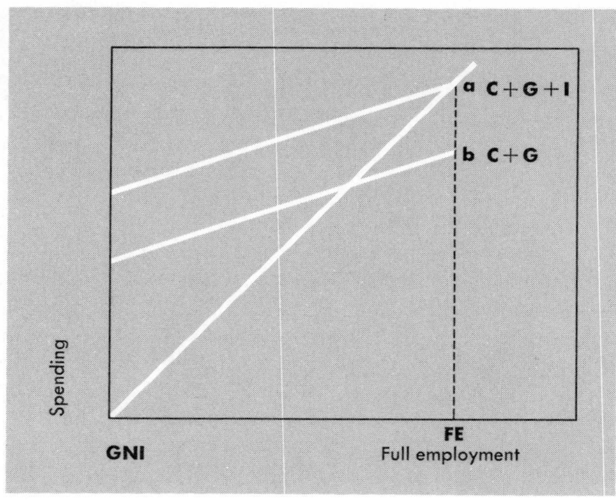

FIG. 6-9 Rate of investment required for full employment.

Thus, monetary policy is one of a set of instruments which can be used in achieving the full employment goal. The appropriate use of any one instrument of policy depends on the way in which the other policies are used.

For any given fiscal policy, some particular rate of investment is required to achieve full employment. The line $C + G$ in Fig. 6-9 shows the consumption

FIG. 6-10 Money supply required for a full employment rate of investment.

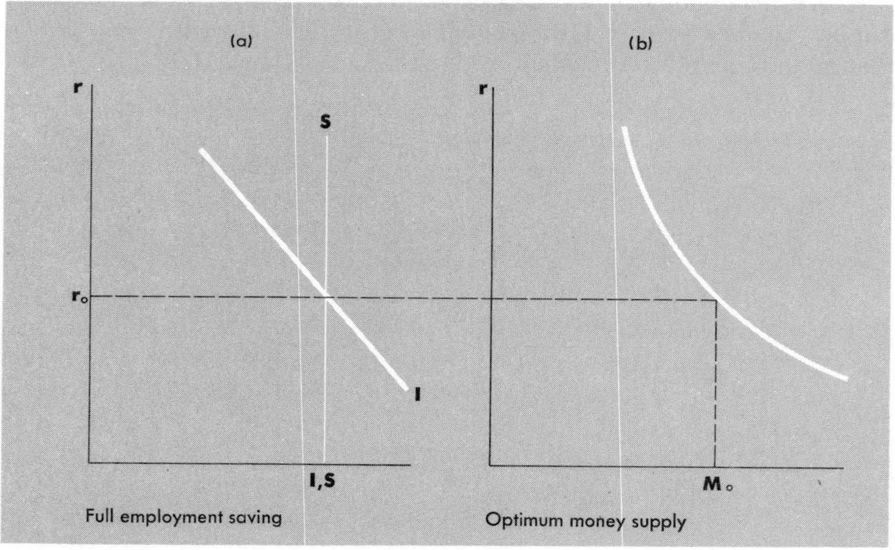

plus government expenditure at any level of income resulting from a particular combination of government expenditures and taxes. Given that fiscal policy, the task of monetary policy is to produce an investment demand which makes $C + G + I$ pass through point a above FE. Tighter money would generate too much unemployment.

The distance ba—the excess of full-employment income over consumption and government expenditures at full employment—is the potential *full employment saving* of the economy. It represents the volume of private saving that would take place at full employment, plus government saving (which may be positive or negative). The task of monetary policy is to find a level of interest rates which exactly equates investment demand with full-employment saving. For if the monetary authorities can manage the money supply so this interest rate will result, the economy will actually achieve full employment.

The problem facing the monetary authority is illustrated in Fig. 6-10. Line I in (a) shows the level of investment associated with different levels of interest rates out of full-employment income. The vertical line S shows full employment saving. The interest rate which will make investment equal saving at a full-employment income is r_0. The curve marked Mfe in Fig. 6-10 (b) is the demand for money at a full-employment income level. A money supply of M_0 is necessary to achieve the interest rate r_0. In the absence of conflicts with other objectives, such as price stability, M_0 is the proper amount of money supply which the Federal Reserve should attempt to provide, given a fiscal policy.

Suppose it is desired to raise the growth of potential by increasing the rate of investment (and hence of saving). Note that the level of full-employment saving depends not only on the level of full-employment income but also on the fiscal policy adopted. Full-employment saving can be increased by cutting government expenditures or by raising taxes. Monetary policy can then be eased to lower interest rates, induce more investment, and thereby increase the rate of growth of output. Thus, the mix of fiscal and monetary policies will affect the rate of growth of potential.

Of course, if fiscal policy is made more restrictive without a corresponding easing of monetary policy, the result will not be more saving and growth, but a decline in total demand and GNP.

THE NEED FOR A GROWING MONEY SUPPLY

At any one moment there is a correct level of interest rates and money supply for the existing fiscal policy. But of course the level of money supply required to produce full employment is always changing. As our labor force increases, technology improves, capital is accumulated, the full employment GNP increases. Full employment saving will increase along with the full employment GNP. The rate of investment corresponding to a full employment level of income and any rate of interest will rise. In Fig. 6-10 the rise in the full employment level of income over time would shift both the *I* curve and the *S* curve to the right. They may continue to intersect at about the same level of interest rates. (The movement of the investment curve depends on many other factors besides the change in income. So the rightward shift in the investment curve might be greater or less than the shift in the full employment savings curve.)

The demand-for-money curve also shifts to the right with a higher level of income. So to keep the interest rate about the same and to assure investment of the increasing full employment saving, the money supply has to increase through time.

why money supply has to increase

MONETARY POLICY AND RESOURCE ALLOCATION

At the end of Chapter 5, we mentioned that the capital markets work so that the funds flowing into the capital market are allocated to those who are willing to pay the most for them. But how much is available in the capital market? Is there a fixed amount of savings to be allocated? We know that there is not. An increase in investment will raise the level of income and of savings. From your study of national income determination, you know that the rate of saving is equal to investment. There is no fixed amount of savings to be allocated among competing investors.

The amount of savings that *should* be allocated among investors is the amount people are willing to save at a full employment level of income. (If the Federal Reserve provides the right amount of money, a full employment income will actually be achieved.) The amount of savings generated by that level of income will be efficiently allocated if the rest of the capital markets do their job. But if the Federal Reserve doesn't provide enough money, there will be waste. Some potential investors will be priced out of the market even though there are idle resources.

Thus, generally, it is the job of monetary policy to assure the right total amount of investment and to leave to the market how the new capital is allocated to different uses. Some critics have argued that monetary policy is not completely neutral among uses, however. Much of the impact of tighter money and higher interest rates seems to fall on home building, a particularly long-lived form of investment and one extremely dependent on borrowing in the capital market for financing. The fixed investments of many large corporations that are able to finance wholly out of internal sources—their retained earnings and depreciation allowances—are likely to be affected little or not at all. Other investors fall in between: many large and small businesses do wish to finance part of their investments by borrowing, and state and local governments issue bonds to pay for many of their public works such as schools, hospitals, and roads. Government has taken steps to make the impact of monetary policy more even by initiating special lending programs for housing, small business, and agriculture.

MONEY AND INCOME IN MOVEMENT

So far we have examined the influence of the money supply on the equilibrium level of income under a fixed set of conditions. But the world we observe is one of growth and change. In that world there is continuous interaction between changes in the money supply and changes in the many other forces working on the level of income and expenditure. It is useful to trace out at least a few steps in that interaction process.

Suppose that, for some reason, the rate of expenditure on goods and services starts to rise while the money supply remains constant. Government expenditures, for example, might have increased with no change in tax rates. As a result of the greater government purchases, there will be an increase in the rate of flow of income to households and businesses, and they in turn will tend to increase their rates of expenditure. Thus there is a tendency for all the elements of gross national product (GNP) to move upward: consumption (C) and investment (I), as well as government spending (G) participate in this trend. An initial rise in G will lead directly and indirectly to an increase in GNP. With M (money supply) constant, an increase in GNP leads to a rise in interest rates.

The sequence may be put in the following schematic way:

$$\begin{array}{ccccccc} +G & \rightarrow & +I & \rightarrow & +\text{GNP} & \rightarrow & +r \\ & \searrow & +C & \nearrow & & & \end{array}$$

where r is the interest rate and the plus sign indicates a positive change.

We have shown that an increase in expenditure occurring when the supply of money is constant leads to an increase in interest rates, but of course the money supply does not have to be absolutely constant. If income rises by 10 per cent and the money supply by 5 per cent, for example, interest rates are likely to rise.

We can now expand our causal sequence to take into account the effect of rising interest rates. We add a term $+ r \rightarrow - I$ to represent the adverse effect of the rise in interest rates on the rate of investment. The entire sequence now is:

$$\begin{array}{ccccccccc} +G & \rightarrow & +I & \rightarrow & +\text{GNP} & \rightarrow & +r & \rightarrow & -I \\ & \searrow & +C & \nearrow & & & & & \end{array}$$

The negative change in investment induced by the rise in interest rates offsets some of the positive acceleration effect of the initial rise in income on investment.

Thus the failure of the money supply to grow acts a brake on the income increase that was induced by the growth in government expenditures. Of course, it does not make any difference whether the sequence is started by an increase in government expenditure or by an increase in private expenditure. The initial force leading to greater expenditures might come from a change in technology or in the rate of population growth or from some other factor favorable to private investment. The sequence would then be:

$$+I \rightarrow +I \rightarrow +\text{GNP} \rightarrow +r \rightarrow -I$$
$$\searrow +C \nearrow$$

Notice that investment, *I*, appears in the sequence three times: first, because the initial spending impulse was in the investment area; second, because an increase in income always encourages investment; third, because an increase in interest rates checks investment. The sequence would continue further of course. The decline of investment would reduce GNP, and so on, and so on.

The sequence could even start with consumption if there were, say, a tax reduction for households. It makes no difference where the initial spending impulse comes from. If the money supply does not increase, the last term in the sequence will always be a negative force working on investment.

We have said that a constant money supply operates as a brake, slowing down the growth of expenditure. How effective a brake is it? No general answer is possible. Under some circumstances the monetary brake could be very weak and ineffective. Under others it could be strong enough to prevent income from rising at all without an increase in *M*. The strength of the brake depends on the relative response of demand for money and investment to the interest rate. Suppose, for example, that (1) it is very easy to induce households and businesses to take substitutes for money (e.g., savings deposits and Treasury bills) in response to a small rise in interest rates; and (2) investment is very insensitive to interest rates. Then a strong impulse toward increasing spending (e.g., an increase in government expenditure or a change in various factors favorable to investment) could drive income up considerably but would increase the interest rate only slightly. And the "negative feedback" of the increase in interest rates would have little adverse effect on investment.

But if those interest-rate responses were the reverse, a fixed money supply would choke off any tendency for income to rise. Suppose that (1) demand for money were very insensitive to interest rates, and (2) investment were very sensitive to interest rates. Then a slight rise in income would cause a large rise in interest rates, which would reduce investment sufficiently to offset the initial impulse to rising income. Of course, the real situation is always somewhere in between. We will discuss some concrete cases illustrating the operation of the monetary brake in the next chapter.

ANOTHER APPROACH: THE QUANTITY THEORY OF MONEY

We have been discussing the impact of money on expenditures in terms of changes in the supply and demand for money holdings. It is also possible to think about the effects of the money supply on expenditures in terms of the rate of movement of money. People receive money, hold it for a while, then spend it. We may ask one of two questions: How much money do people want to hold at a given level of income and interest rates? How quickly do people spend money after they receive it? The second approach, stressing the velocity of money, has a long intellectual history, going back at least to David Hume in the 1750's. National income analysis has superseded it in the last three decades, but the older approach continues to have its adherents and is indeed having a strong revival.

Measuring the Speed of Money Movement

We can't watch individual dollars move, but we can measure how fast money moves on the average. In 1970 there were *$10 trillion* worth of money transactions in the U.S. The average amount of money in that year—coins, currency, and checking accounts—was \$200 billion. So each dollar changed hands about 50 times on the average. The ratio of the volume of transactions to the stock of money is called the *transactions velocity of money*.

Since we are interested primarily in the relation between money and the output of goods and services, it is also desirable to have a measure of the relation of the stock of money to the annual flow of final purchases of goods and services—the gross national product. The ratio of GNP to the stock of money, $\frac{GNP}{M}$, is called the *income velocity of money* (denoted by V). In 1970 the GNP was \$976 billion, so $V = \frac{976}{209} = 4.2$ per year for 1970. The income velocity of money differs from the transactions velocity because it excludes (1) financial transactions and (2) intermediate transactions; that is, has counted the payment to the dealer for the finished automobile but left out the dealer's payment to the manufacturer, the manufacturer's payment for steel, and so on.

Income velocity is sometimes called circuit velocity because it measures the times per year that a dollar completes the circuit from income to purchase of goods and services and back to income again.

The income velocity of money may be defined by the equation $V \equiv \frac{\text{GNP}}{M}$ where the three-bar equality sign indicates that the equation is definitional. It's always true because it only restates the definition of V. We can rewrite the equation by splitting GNP into its components—prices and outputs. The *value* of the goods and services produced in a year is the product of the physical output of goods and services (O) and their price level (P). So GNP $= P \times O$. The equation $MV \equiv P \times O$ is called the "equation of exchange."

Since the equation is essentially a definition, it doesn't tell us anything about the real world. But it does serve to remind us of some connections between money and other things that must always be true. In particular, any increase in M must be accompanied by either a decrease in V or an increase in GNP expenditures and an increase in output, prices, or both.

If V were constant, control of the money supply would mean direct control of national income and expenditure. An increase in M would imply a proportional rise in price level or in level of output, or in some combination of the two. Moreover, since the potential output of the economy is limited at any time, any very large and rapid increase in M would necessarily produce a more or less proportionate rise in prices. Any substantial contraction in M would spell depression, with declining output and employment and a falling price level. But remember that those conclusions are valid *only if V is constant*. The notion that the level of expenditure and the price level are simply related to the amount of money in existence is called the *quantity theory of money*.

Actually V varies a good deal. Look at Fig. 6–11. You can see that in 1945 the average dollar went around the income circuit about twice. In 1929 and 1965 the average dollar went around the income circuit about four times a year.

It still may be possible to use the quantity theory approach. We could analyze income flows in terms of the movements of M *and* the movements of V. Thus movements in V may be caused by changes in the way payments are made. Money moves more quickly if people are paid weekly instead of monthly, because people hold less money for ordinary day-to-day transactions. Or velocity may change because of varying levels of confidence. If people hold money idle because of fear of unemployment, the average rate of movement of money will decline.

Thus we could try to explain GNP by explaining the movements of M and the movements of V. And monetary policy would be directed toward (1) increasing M in pace with the growth of potential GNP, and (2) offsetting movements of V by increasing the supply of money when V declined, and vice versa. The approach will not work, however, if changes in M or changes

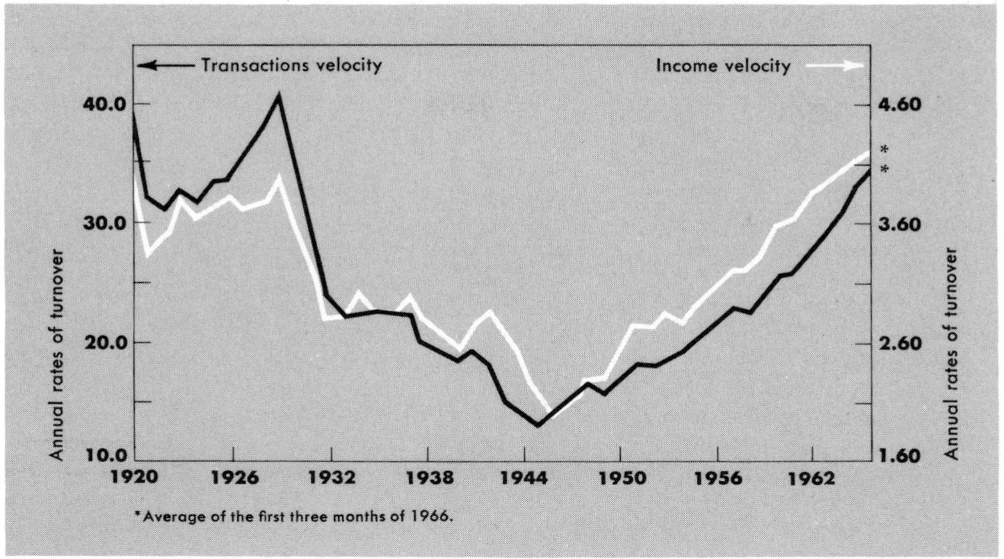

FIG. 6-11 The velocity of money, 1920–1966. (Source: St. Louis Federal Reserve Bank, Research Dept.)

in GNP *cause* changes in *V*. In that case the movements of *V* do not cause movements in GNP but reflect them.

Most economists think that is the typical situation. Velocity moves in the same general way as the interest rate (see Fig. 6–12). Most economists explain the movement of velocity in relation to the interest rate in terms of the theory of demand for money outlined above.

If GNP rises, demand for money increases. If the supply of money does not rise or does not rise as fast as income, interest rates rise. A rise in GNP relative to *M is* an increase in *V*. The accompanying rise in interest rates is necessary to induce households and businesses to accommodate their demands for money to the available supply. Similarly, a rise in *M* causes a decline in interest rates and, simultaneously, a fall in *V*. If changes in *M* and GNP cause changes in *V*, then we can neither treat *V* as constant nor regard it as an explanation of changes in GNP.

THE NEW QUANTITY THEORY

That argument and the observed variations in *V* convinced most economists that the quantity theory of money as stated above could not provide a satisfactory basis for controlling the level of demand. But in recent years, a number of economists have restated the quantity theory. Whereas the

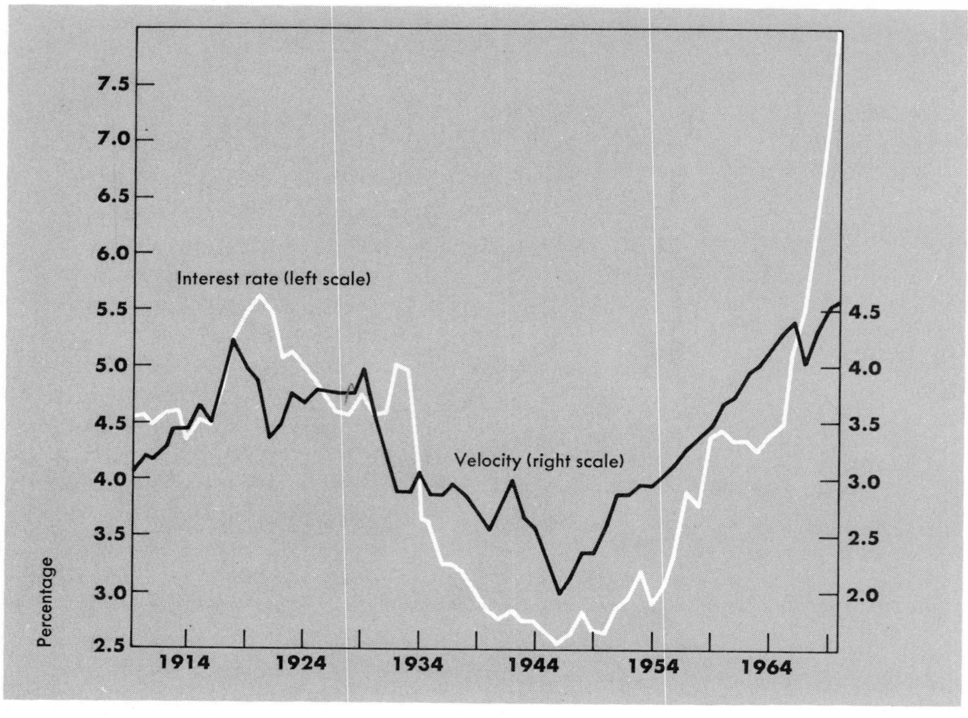

FIG. 6-12 Annual income velocity compared with corporate bond yields, 1909–1970. (Source: H. A. Latane, "Income Velocity and Interest Rates," *The Review of Economics and Statistics*, November, 1960. 1959–1970: *Economic Report of the President*, January, 1971.)

old quantity theory ran in terms of the relation between the *level of GNP* and the *stock of money*, the new quantity theory is usually stated in terms of the relation between *changes in the stock of money* and *changes in GNP*. Milton Friedman, the best-known proponent of the new quantity theory or monetarist approach, has massed much evidence to show that, on the average, rapid increases in M are accompanied or followed by relatively rapid increases in GNP. His studies cover the business cycle record over the past century. More recently, the staff of the Federal Reserve Bank of St. Louis has published a number of studies showing an association between short-run changes in money supply and short-run changes in GNP. The St. Louis Bank staff has also made a number of relatively successful predictions of GNP changes in the past few years. Their evidence has set off a fierce controversy among economists. The controversy is not merely an academic one. Followers of the monetarist approach argue that monetary policy rather than fiscal policy should be the dominant instrumental control of aggregate demand. Moreover, they want monetary policy to be conducted in terms of rates of change of money supply alone rather than in terms of interest rates, and credit conditions. These policy questions are discussed in Chapter 8.

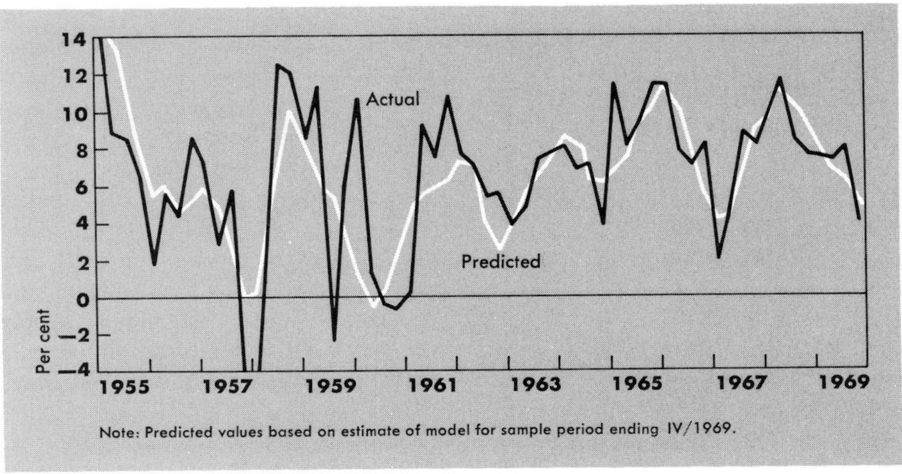

FIG. 6-13 Annual rates of change in GNP and predicted GNP. (Source: St. Louis Federal Reserve Bank.)

An example of the evidence provided by the St. Louis Federal Reserve Bank is shown in Fig. 6–13, which shows the annual changes in GNP from 1955 to 1969 compared with the changes derived from a weighted average of earlier changes in money supply (demand deposits and currency). The association is impressive, although it leaves much of the change in GNP unexplained and the association is far better in the later years than in the earlier ones. This and other similar studies have greatly strengthened the case of the new quantity theorists. Others remain doubtful because it is not clear whether the changes in *M* have caused changes in GNP or only accompanied them. They argue that the forces leading to an expansion in GNP may also lead to increased bank lending and an increase in money supply. But the opponents of the monetarist argument have not provided a convincing refutation of the monetarists' evidence.

In any case, it is not clear that the monetarist argument (except in its most extreme form) is inconsistent with the more orthodox analysis running in terms of changes in money supply, induced changes in interest rates and credit conditions, and the effects of such changes on spending. It appears to be so mainly because the monetarists proceed directly from changes in *M* to changes in GNP without going through all the intermediate steps in the process.

Short-Run Changes in V and Interest Rates

As Fig. 6–12 indicates, the velocity of money can be expanded or contracted by changes in interest rates. These changes occur because changes in interest rates induce potential holders of money to switch from demand deposits and currency to interest-bearing substitutes (savings deposits and shares, Treasury bills, etc.). But households and businesses do not change their money-holding practices very quickly. A rise of one-fourth in interest rates from say 4 per cent to 5 per cent may produce a more or less proportional rise in velocity from say 3 to 3.75 per year. But the rise in velocity may occur gradually over a period of several years. In the short run, a rather large change in interest rates may be required to produce a modest increase in velocity.

If large changes in interest rates are required to induce quick changes in velocity, the growth of the money supply can have a powerful influence on the short-run swings in the economy. The growth rate of the money supply can be thought of as interacting with fiscal policy and other forces influencing demand—sometimes reinforcing them, sometimes offsetting them, sometimes remaining neutral.

1. When nonmonetary factors tend to make GNP grow rapidly, a relatively large increase in M is required to keep interest rates from rising. If that large increase occurs, the full force of the nonmonetary forces will be felt and both GNP and M will grow rapidly. But if the money supply does not grow rapidly, interest rates will rise and part of the expansion of GNP will be choked off.

2. When nonmonetary forces tend to make demand grow slowly, only a small increase in M is required to maintain constant interest rates. If there is a small increase in M, we will observe slow growth in GNP and slow growth in M. If M increases relatively rapidly, interest rates will fall and the weakness in other factors will be partly offset by the rapid rise in M.

3. Finally, if nonmonetary forces lead to an average growth in GNP, an average growth rate for M will be required to keep interest rates constant. If M grows at an above-average rate, interest rates will fall and GNP will grow at an above-average rate. If M grows at a below-average rate, interest rates will rise and GNP will rise at a below-average rate.

As a result of these conditions, one would expect a positive but not perfect association between growth of M and growth of GNP. Notice that the association between rate of growth of M and rate of growth of GNP is strongest in the last case. If nonmonetary forces vary little, monetary policy has the greatest influence on the economy.

In fact, of course, the situation is more complicated because monetary policy works with a fairly long lag. As we would expect, the strongest association is found between changes in M at one time and changes in GNP at a later time.

The results obtained by the new quantity theory method are not basically inconsistent with the more complex analysis of the income expenditure approach, wherein we attempt to trace step by step all the different ways in which changes in Federal Reserve actions interact with other determinants of spending for goods and services. Because those processes are complex and changing, some monetary impacts may be overlooked or underestimated. The velocity-based models, by contrast, rely on the proposition that when money supply does not grow fast enough to accommodate the growth of demand, something has to give. But they do not attempt to specify exactly what has to give at every point in time.

On the other hand, the causal significance of the data used by the new quantity theorists remains ambiguous. In some cases, it seems clear that a change in the growth of the money supply has been the active cause of an acceleration or retardation in the growth of GNP. In others, it appears that other forces stimulated an accelerated growth of demand while the Federal Reserve permitted a more rapid growth of money supply to accommodate the increased demand for money. In the latter cases it is not clear that the increase in the growth of money supply alone—that is, in the absence of other expansionary forces—would have brought about an equally rapid growth of demand. There is, therefore, some reason to believe that the quantity theorists' equation may exaggerate the causal impact of changes in money supply.

Economists and statisticians continue to dispute these ambiguities and will continue to do so until events provide the data to resolve their conflicts.

The monetarist approach provides a different way of demonstrating that changes in monetary policy have a substantial influence on economic events. But its real significance lies in its influence on the conduct of practical monetary policy. In the next chapter we review the conduct of monetary policy in the decades following World War II.

SUMMARY

Interest rates are determined by the interaction of supply and demand for money. The supply of money is determined by the actions of the Federal Reserve System. The demand for money at *a given interest rate* rises with the level of income and the level of wealth. As income and wealth grow, both businesses and households want more money for (1) day-to-day transactions, (2) contingencies, and (3) as a safe element in their stock of wealth.

The amount of money people want to hold at a *given level of income and wealth* declines as the interest rate rises. When interest rates rise, businesses and households find it worthwhile to hold interest-earning substitutes for money, such as saving deposits, instead of holding demand deposits and currency.

The level of interest rates influences the level of investment. A rise in interest rates discourages investment and a fall in interest rates stimulates investment. The rate of investment expenditures is a major determinant of the level of GNP.

To attain a full-employment GNP, the level of interest rates must be just high enough to bring about a rate of investment equal to the amount the public wishes to save at a full-employment GNP. (Saving includes government saving, which may be positive or negative.)

If we are to achieve a full-employment level of GNP, the money supply must equal the amount the public wishes to hold at the level of interest rates required to generate enough investment to absorb full-employment saving.

If the public wishes to save more at a given level of income, the money supply should increase to reduce interest rates and increase the rate of investment, thereby maintaining full employment.

The full-employment level of income grows from year to year, with growth in the labor force and its productivity. The demand for money grows with income and, ordinarily, the supply of money must also grow. Otherwise, interest rates would tend to rise and check the growth of investment.

Many factors influence the level of GNP. A rise in GNP may be stimulated by an increase in investment opportunities, by an increase in government expenditures, or by a reduction in tax rates. An increase in income from any of those sources sets off a multiplier process. At the same time, the rise in income is a further stimulus to investment. If the money supply does not increase, the increase in interest rates acts as a brake which slows or stops the growth of income by depressing investment.

On the other hand, an increase in the money supply can stimulate investment and cause a rise in income. Thus monetary policy can be used either to check or to encourage the growth of demand.

Monetary Policy in Practice

CHAPTER SEVEN

In Chapter 3 we showed how the Federal Reserve can regulate the supply of money by means of its control over required reserve ratios and the volume of bank reserves. The Federal Reserve System, you will recall, was brought into existence as a solution to the monetary problems of the national banking system. To that end it was granted wide powers: to issue currency, to buy and sell securities, to lend to member banks at varying interest rates, and to vary reserve requirements. Those powers enable the Federal Reserve System to control the money supply. The System was supposed to act as a shock absorber—to absorb or offset the impact of various factors, such as seasonal variations in demand for currency, which had hitherto disturbed the banking system. It was widely believed that the banking panics of the period preceding World War I were a major cause of economic instability and that those panics were caused by the mechanical defects of the national banking system. The basic notion was that the Federal Reserve System could "keep money out of the way."

But "keeping money out of the way" has not proved to be enough. Even when there are no undesirable fluctuations in bank reserves, and even assuming that the causes of bank failures in the 1930's have been removed, problems remain. There is no doubt that undesirable changes in bank reserves and bank failures contributed greatly to economic instability in the past. But plenty of causes of instability remain.

Private investment demand is still influenced by a number of factors—population changes, changes in techniques, the development of new products, and changing locational factors. Moreover, because the rate of investment is influenced by the level of profits and the rate of capacity utilization, any rapid increase in income tends to generate further increases in investment. On the other hand, investment creates capacity, and investment will tend to decline if income does not grow to keep pace with the capacity being created. Variations in government expenditures may sometimes offset other sources of variations in income, but at times changes in government expenditures (e.g., those due to wars) may be destabilizing in themselves. Consumer expenditures tend to follow changes in income, resulting in the multiplier; but at times there are booms and slumps in durable goods expenditures, which are an independent source of instability.

Under the impact of these forces, the rate of change of total expenditure for goods and services tends to vary widely from year to year. When expenditures grow slowly, the rate of increase of output is also slow and falls below the rate of growth of potential output. Then idle capacity accumulates and the rate of unemployment rises. At other times, expenditures rise more rapidly than the rate of growth of potential output. Unless there is slack, prices will rise.[1] Moreover, rising prices and a rate of growth of output that cannot be sustained in the long run may lead to speculative investment based on unrealistic assumptions about future sales and profits. The inevitable collapse of a speculative investment boom is likely to have an adverse effect on the whole economy, including sectors not involved in the boom.

Almost everyone agrees that the objective of monetary policy should be to reduce the instability caused by the factors just mentioned. When expenditures for goods and services are falling or rising too slowly, monetary policy should be used to encourage investment and increase the rate of growth of expenditure. When, on the other hand, expenditure is growing too rapidly, monetary policy should be used to brake expenditures.

So far so good, but there the agreement ends. People disagree about the importance of inflation and about the extent to which it can be influenced by changes in aggregate demand. They disagree about the degree of danger from speculative booms. And in periods of high unemployment, people disagree about the extent to which unemployment can be influenced by changes in aggregate demand. Everyone is for all the good things and against all the bad things, however, that does not help much.

But, let us go on. In this chapter let us continue our discussion of how Federal Reserve policy has actually operated in recent years and the effect it has had on economic activity.

[1] See C. L. Schultze, *National Income Analysis,* 3rd ed., for a discussion of these problems.

INSTRUMENTS AND ORGANIZATION OF MONETARY POLICY

The Federal Reserve System influences economic activity through three major policy instruments each controlled in a different way. They are

1. Varying reserve requirements.
2. Open-market operations.
3. Varying the discount rate.

Open-market operations are the ordinary means of changing bank reserves. Reserve ratios are changed only when a particularly large change in money supply is desired or when the Board wants to use this change to announce a shift in monetary policy.

Open-market operations are carried on continuously. In order to offset currency and gold movements and other factors affecting bank reserves, the System must buy or sell securities almost every day. Decisions on the objectives of open-market operations are made by the Federal Open Market Committee (F.O.M.C.). This committee consists of the seven members of the Board of Governors, the president of the Federal Reserve Bank of New York, and the presidents of four of the other reserve banks in rotation. The F.O.M.C. usually meets every three weeks. The committee considers the economic outlook and decides whether open-market operations should aim at making credit a little cheaper and easier to get or a little more expensive and hard to get. Their decision is summed up in a directive to the New York Federal Reserve Bank. The New York Federal Reserve Bank makes the actual purchases and sales indicated by the F.O.M.C. There is daily telephone consultation between the staff of the Board and that of the N. Y. Bank.

Discount rates are set by the directors of the 12 Federal Reserve Banks. But the rates they set must be approved by the Board of Governors. Usually all the banks change their rates at once (or within a few days), but occasionally one bank may lag behind the others.

Since the early 1960's the Federal Reserve System's regulation of interest rates on time and savings deposits (regulation *Q*) has become important. The Board of Governors has used the ceiling rates on consumer time and savings deposits to limit the competition between banks and thrift institutions. The ceiling rates on large certificates of deposit have been used to prevent banks from bidding for funds on the open market. It was hoped that this measure would restrict bank lending to business and thereby reduce business investment. However, banks found ways to raise funds in spite of the regulation.

The Federal Reserve also has at its disposal several minor instruments of policy. They are confined to specific situations and do not affect the money supply and credit conditions as strongly as the general instruments. But at times their use can be important, and they add flexibility to monetary policy.

The Federal Reserve has power to set *margin requirements* on stock market credit: a purchaser of stocks has to put up a certain percentage in cash (this percentage has varied from 50 to 90 per cent in recent years), and the rest can be financed by a broker's loan. This regulation is designed to avoid the kind of excesses in the stock market that have led to disaster in the past. The Federal Reserve uses this power very sparingly to avoid the charge of manipulating the stock market.

The Federal Reserve also utilizes the so-called *jawbone*. In periods when restraint on bank lending is desirable, the Federal Reserve may appeal to the commercial banks to scrutinize loan applications particularly carefully and to emphasize those loans which will add to production. It may seek to discourage loans for inventory hoarding or financial speculation. Although such preaching by public officials is rarely effective for long unless backed by other measures, the Federal Reserve, through its ability to withhold the discount privilege, has considerable powers of persuasion over the commercial banks.

The voluntary approach to monetary policy reached a high point in the *Guidelines for Foreign Bank Lending* adopted by the Federal Reserve Board at the request of the President in 1965. These Guidelines "request" commercial banks not to increase their total loans outside the United States by more than a small percentage specified each year. During its initial years, this program was a highly successful means of improving our international balance of payments.

Earlier in the postwar period, the Federal Reserve had at its command a number of other selective credit control powers. During the Korean War it could set minimum down-payment requirements and maximum repayment periods on consumer credit for automobiles and other durables. It had similar powers over the terms of mortgages. But in general, the Federal Reserve has favored the general rather than the selective approach to monetary control. The Federal Reserve preferred to let the capital market allocate the total volume of investment into its most profitable uses. It sought to keep monetary policy impersonal, and let the market, rather than the Board's own choice of instruments, determine which sector of the economy would be most severely restricted in its access to credit.

In recent years, however, the Board has been forced to recognize that its actions do have disproportionate effects on important sectors of the economy. As noted earlier, it has attempted to use the ceiling rates on time deposits to lessen the impact of monetary restraint on housing and to increase the impact on business investment. Some governors have proposed this use of more direct credit controls.

MONETARY POLICY AFTER WORLD WAR II

From the end of World War II until 1951, Federal Reserve policy was oriented toward helping the Treasury solve its financial problems. During World War II, the Federal Reserve had agreed to assist the Treasury by maintaining a fixed schedule of interest rates. The Federal Reserve stood ready to buy or sell unlimited quantities of government securities at fixed interest yields (long-term bonds at 2.5 per cent, 90-day Treasury bills at 1.25 per cent, and so on). Thus the Federal Reserve was prepared to create whatever amount of reserves was needed to supply the money the public wanted at those fixed interest rates. The government attempted to limit the inflationary pressure generated by its huge expenditures by a vast array of direct controls—rationing, price control, allocation of raw materials, and direct controls on business and consumer borrowing. At the end of the war, as controls were dismantled, the Federal Reserve sought to free itself from the Treasury. For several years, however, the Treasury—with presidential support—resisted any change. Treasury officials feared a sharp rise in interest rates and a fall in bond prices. The fall in bond prices after World War I had caused a great public outcry, because many unsophisticated investors had bought Liberty Bonds during the war. Finally, in 1950, after long negotiations, the Federal Reserve and the Treasury reached an accord. The Federal Reserve regained its basic control over monetary policy in return for an understanding that it would try to prevent "disorderly conditions" in the government securities market.

The period when interest rates were "pegged" by the Federal Reserve is interesting to monetary analysts because it was a unique experiment in control or noncontrol of the money supply. During that period, the money supply can hardly be said to have "caused" any changes in demand, since it was itself completely responsive to the demands of the public. The rate of change of GNP varied a good deal during the period between the end of the war and the accord, and it is difficult to explain these variations in terms of money supply variations. Pegging interest rates is not likely to be tried again but as we shall see, there have been other periods when it must be said that the growth of the money supply was determined by the Federal Reserve's desire to provide enough money to limit if not prevent a rise in interest rates.

THE CYCLICAL PATTERN OF FEDERAL RESERVE POLICY: 1951–1961

During the fifties, Federal Reserve policy again became an active factor in determining the pace of economic activity. But although the Federal Reserve was more active than in preceding decades, its officials did not suppose that they could, or should, take responsibility for controlling or determining the growth of demand. Broadly speaking, the System pursued a policy aimed at moderating the swings in economic activity. During the decade following the accord, concern over inflation alternated with concern over excessive unemployment. Three periods of economic expansion alternated with three recessions. In each of the upswings—1950–1953, 1954–1957, and 1958–1960—the System aimed, by its own account, at checking the growth of expenditures in order to prevent inflation and the development of an unstable speculative boom. In those instances, it used its powers to limit the availability and raise the cost of credit. During recessions, on the other hand, the System sought to reduce the cost of credit and make it more readily available.

Policy Actions in Recession

Federal Reserve policy was clear-cut and easy to follow during the recessions of 1953–1954, 1957–1958, and 1960–1961. In each of those periods the discount rate was reduced several times; required reserve ratios were reduced three times in each of the recession periods. Open-market operations were used to offset other factors affecting reserves but were not used as the primary instrument in encouraging increases in the money supply.

Policy Actions During Upswings

During the upswings of 1954–1957 and 1958–1960, Federal Reserve policy assumed a quite different character. The discount rate was raised several times in each of these periods to keep it above rising market interest rates and so help to limit member-bank borrowing. Required reserve ratios were left unchanged. During the 1958–1960 period, open-market operations were used mainly to offset the restrictive effects of gold outflows and increasing currency demands. The net effect of open-market operations, together with the other factors mentioned, was to reduce bank reserves only slightly.

THE EARLY 1960's: FACILITATING EXPANSION

The recession of 1960–1961 ended, for a time, the seesaw struggle between inflation and unemployment. During this period unemployment rose to 7 per cent and remained over 5 per cent until mid-1965. Prices were relatively stable during the whole period, and almost everyone agreed that the objective of policy should be to promote a rapid growth of GNP until full employment was reached again. Fiscal policy was generally expansive, though only moderately so, until the 1964 tax cut.

From a domestic standpoint, there was every reason for an expansionary monetary policy, but the persisting balance-of-payments deficit was a restraining factor.

In these circumstances, monetary policy was aimed at permitting a rapid expansion of demand to continue without any restraint from rising interest rates (on bonds, mortgages, or bank loans) or from the kind of restraint on bank lending that had occurred during earlier expansions. The balance-of-payments problem prevented the Federal Reserve from seeking a marked reduction in interest rates and even made a rise in the shortest-term interest rates desirable.

During the early 1960's open-market operations provided enough reserves to permit a continuous expansion in the money supply. But since the money supply did not expand as fast as the GNP, short-term interest rates tended to rise. The discount rate was raised several times to keep it roughly in line with market rates.

The Federal Reserve also raised the ceiling rate on time deposits several times during the same period. Those moves, together with the development of negotiable certificates of deposits, made it possible for banks to attract a large volume of time and savings deposits. Thus, while short-term rates rose because of the limited increase in demand deposits, banks were able to accommodate the increasing demand for business loans without facing the difficulties they had experienced in the upswing periods of the 1950's. Banks were able to buy large amounts of securities, mainly state and local issues, and they could accommodate their business loan customers, as well. As a result, credit was readily available and long-term interest rates were relatively stable in spite of the upward pressure on short rates.

MONETARY POLICY DURING THE WAR IN VIET NAM

The expansion of military activity in Viet Nam in the last half of 1965 brought out in acute form all the conflicts and uncertainties involved in the making of monetary policy. In mid-1965, the American economy appeared to be in a very healthy position. Output was expanding rapidly and, after years of excessive unemployment, it seemed that the unemployment rate could be brought down to 4 per cent—the figure generally regarded as an acceptable, if not perfectly satisfactory, definition of full employment. At the same time, prices were rising at a relatively slow rate. It appeared that a satisfactory compromise between the goals of high employment and stable prices could be achieved.

The expansion of the war in Viet Nam changed the picture completely. Even before military orders and expenditures had begun to increase, businesses stepped up their plans to spend money for plant and equipment. Unemployment fell quickly, reaching the 4 per cent level by January 1966, and price increases accelerated.

Throughout the five years from the end of 1965 until the end of 1970, control of inflation was a major concern of Federal Reserve policy. But policy making was complicated by uncertainty over the prospects for restrictive fiscal action and by uncertainty over the effects of the action finally taken in mid-1968 (described below). Moreover, in spite of the salience of the inflation problem, the System had to temper its actions out of concern for the stability of the housing industry and the safety of the nation's financial institutions.

The Federal Reserve's initial reaction to the expansion in Viet Nam was similar to its actions in previous expansions. The discount rate was raised in December 1965 and the creation of reserves was severly limited in the first nine months of 1966.

The conflict between a rapidly expanding economy and a severely restrictive monetary policy led to a rapid rise in interest rates and made it very difficult for banks to accommodate their customers. At the same time, the flow of funds to home building dried up.

By late 1966, it was apparent that restrictive monetary policy supplemented by the belated suspension of the investment tax credit and a rise in the savings rate (whose origin remains a matter of controversy) were producing a sharp reduction in the rate of growth of demand.

The Federal Reserve took the opportunity to move toward an easier policy in order to permit a revival of home building and to unwind the liquidity problems created by the credit crunch of 1966. By summer of 1967, demand was again expanding rapidly under the stimulus of growing federal expenditures. At the same time, however, the President had called for a tax increase and the Federal Reserve, while limiting reserve growth enough to push up interest rates, sought to avoid another crunch. It succeeded in that objective, but meanwhile the growth of demand continued to exceed the growth of potential ouput. Unemployment fell, labor shortages grew more intense, and the price rise accelerated. The income tax surcharge and expenditure limitation finally passed the Congress in June 1968. In the expectation of a quick slow-down following the tax surcharge, the Federal Reserve acted to hold down interest rates in the summer of 1968. But by the time the tax surcharge was passed, inflationary expectations had strengthened. Consumers paid the tax by reducing savings, and business investment continued to grow. By the end of 1968, a return to a severely restrictive policy was necessary.

The 1967–1968 experience again illustrates the problems of monetary policy making. During 1967 and the first part of 1968, monetary policy making had to be based on a forecast of fiscal policy as well as on the behavior of private spenders. Forecasts of private spending in that year were not far off, but the long postponement of tax action posed a continuous dilemma for the Federal Reserve. And, of course, the expansionary actions of the summer of 1968 reflected a major forecasting error. In the light of hindsight, a more restrictive policy in 1967 and 1968 would have saved a great deal of trouble later.

By late 1968, it was apparent that the fiscal package of mid-1968 would not slow the growth of demand as much or as soon as had been expected. Faced with accelerating price increases, and with no immediate relief from inflationary pressures in sight, the Federal Reserve moved to an extremely restrictive policy in 1969. Reserve growth was held down, the discount rate increased, and interest rates rose as usual; but the Federal Reserve refused to raise the ceilings on certificates of deposit.

The combined effect of the return to fiscal restraint in mid-1968 and to monetary restraint late in that year was gradually felt through the year 1969. By the fall it became apparent that the growth of demand had slowed significantly. In 1970 real GNP showed little change, and unemployment had risen to 6 per cent by the end of the year. Monetary policy turned with the economy. The money supply grew by over 5 per cent during 1970 and short-term interest rates fell sharply.

THE EFFECT OF FEDERAL RESERVE POLICY ON MONEY SUPPLY

The policy actions just described influenced the money supply in the way you might expect from what you have learned in Chapters 3 and 4. In each of the recessions, demand deposits expanded rapidly.

However, the expansion was not proportional to the amount of reserves provided through open-market operations and reductions in reserve requirements. At the onset of each of the recessions, member banks were heavily indebted to the Federal Reserve Banks. When additional reserves were made available, the banks which were indebted used part of their reserve gains to repay the Federal Reserve Banks. In addition, some country banks allowed their excess reserves to increase during the downswing (see Fig 7–1). Thus the expansion in demand deposits was not so large as one would expect on the basis of calculations that neglect changes in member-bank borrowing and excess reserves.

During the upswing of 1954–1957, the money supply expanded somewhat, even though reserves were being taken away from the banking system. That was possible because banks reduced their excess reserves and borrowed more from the Federal Reserve Banks. During the upswing of 1958–1960, the money supply rose for a year, then fell as open-market operations shrank bank reserves.

In the long expansion beginning in 1961, the money supply was permitted to grow at a substantially higher rate than during the earlier expansions. This growth in the money supply played a key role in sustaining the expansion. See Fig. 7–2.

From the beginning of 1966 through 1970, the frequent changes in monetary policy created wide swings in the growth of the money supply. Money supply growth came to a halt for a time in the last half of 1966. In

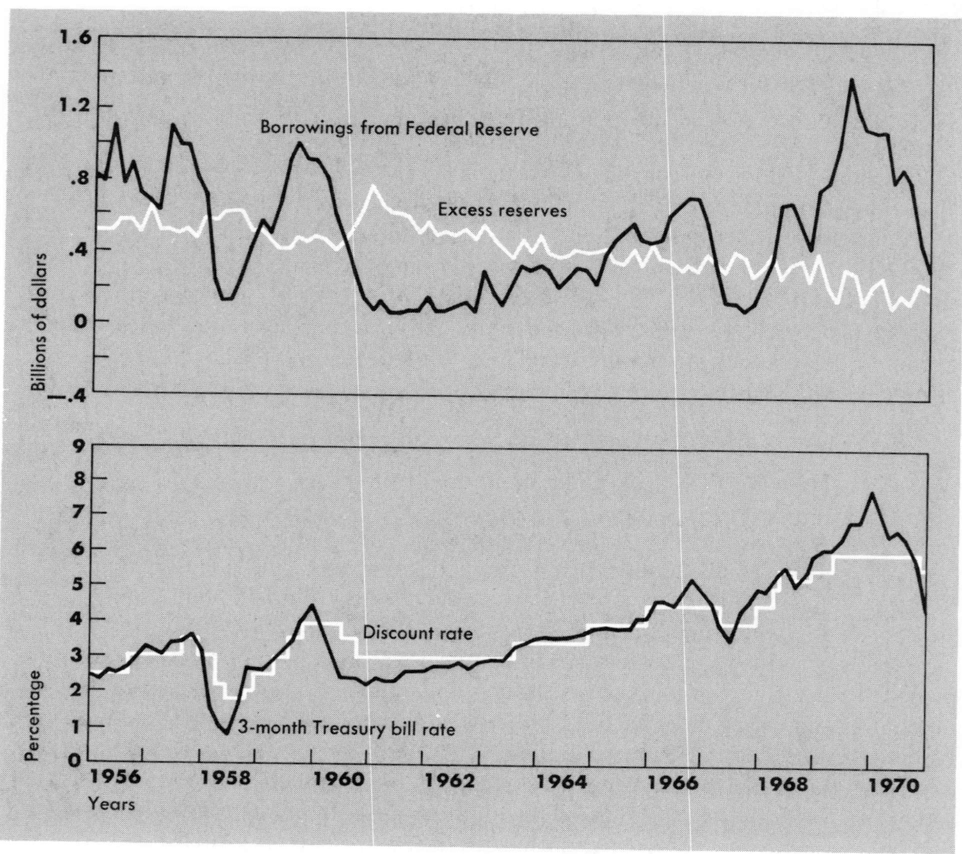

FIG. 7-1 Excess reserves, borrowings, and interest rates. (Source: *Federal Reserve Bulletin.*)

1967 and 1968 the money supply grew at a very rapid rate. The restrictive policy of 1969 then led to another period of slow growth, followed by a resumption of fairly rapid growth in 1970. See Fig. 7–3.

INTEREST-RATE MOVEMENTS

Interest rates have followed a clearly marked cyclical pattern since 1950, declining during recessions and rising during booms. The pattern is readily explained by the movements of GNP and the money supply. During recessions the money supply rose relative to expenditures.

After banks had improved their reserve positions by repaying Federal Reserve loans, they bid for securities, thus lowering interest rates until some individuals found it worthwhile to hold on to money instead of securities.

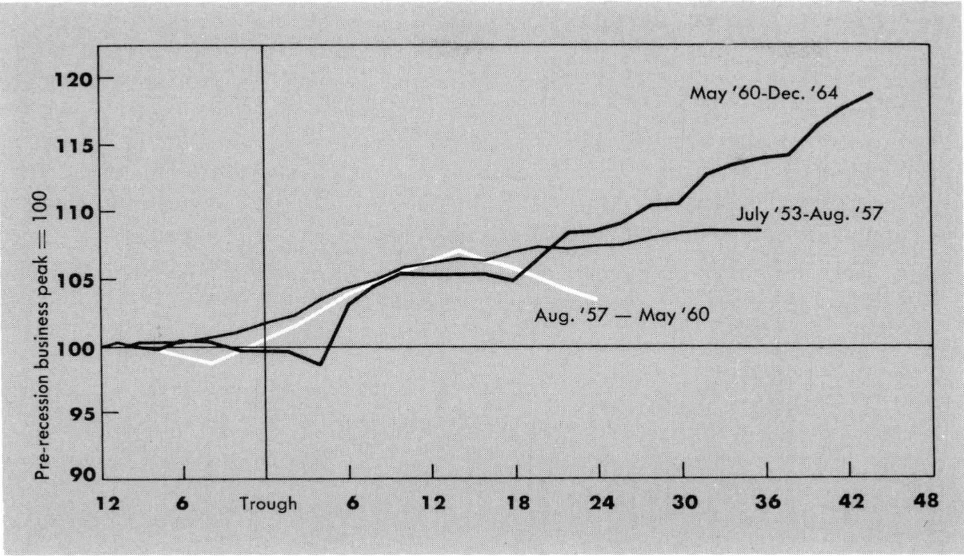

FIG. 7-2 Money supply, seasonally adjusted. Peak and trough months were selected by the National Bureau of Economic Research. (Source: *Federal Reserve Bulletin.*)

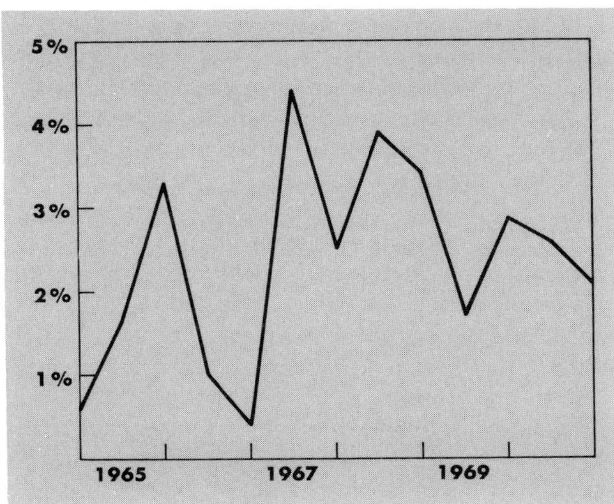

FIG. 7-3 Percentage increase in money supply 1967–1970. (Source: *Federal Reserve Bulletin.*)

During the upswings, the money supply increased slowly or not at all, and the GNP rose relative to the money supply. Businesses and households wanted to hold more money to carry on an increased volume of business. Interest rates had to rise until people who least needed money were induced to buy securities and turn their money over to people who most needed it and were willing to pay for it.

Interest rates generally move together, with the short-term interest rates moving more quickly and swinging over a wider range than the long-term rates. In the early 1960's, however, short-term rates moved up while there was little change in long-term rates. As noted previously, this was due to the new-found ability of banks to increase their short-term liabilities (in the form of time and savings deposits) and acquire longer-term assets, mainly state and local bonds and mortgages.

In the latter half of the 1960's GNP again rose relative to money supply. But the ceiling rates on time deposits prevented banks from creating an effective substitute for demand deposits. The rise in long-term interest rates was probably intensified by expectations of continuing inflationary pressures. In 1969 interest rates reached levels that had not been seen since the Civil War. Rates on medium-grade (Baa) corporate bonds reached 10 per cent.

BANK LOANS AND INVESTMENTS

The managements of commercial banks have had plenty of problems in recent years. They have had to keep adjusting their policies in response to changes in Federal Reserve policy and variations in loan demand.

During recession periods, banks generally repaid their indebtedness to the Federal Reserve and acquired large amounts of state and local securities. In 1958 and 1960 the increase in assets permitted by reductions in reserve ratios was swelled by the increase in savings deposits that occurred during the period when interest rates on bonds were low. Commercial and industrial loans, of course, declined somewhat during the recessions, as did consumer loans.

Bank managements suffered their real headaches during the periods of increasing business activity in 1954–1957 and 1958–1960. They began the upswing periods in a fairly strong position. They were generally out of debt to the Reserve Banks and had large portfolios of United States securities which could be readily sold without loss. But as the upswing in business activity developed, banks found themselves faced with an intense demand for credit, and they experienced considerable difficulty in accommodating their customers. The expansion in loan demand reflected the high rate of inventory investment and the increased purchases of automobiles and other consumer durables.

To take care of increasing loan demand, commercial banks sold $10 billion worth of United States securities between 1954 and 1957 and $7 billion worth during 1959. Each loan made by a bank created a new demand deposit, and each sale of a government security extinguished a deposit. Thus the extension of loans and the sale of securities balanced off, leaving deposits the same.

But at the same time, the banking system as a whole was losing reserves as a result of Federal Reserve action and the other factors that affect reserves. The banks which suffered a net loss of reserves then used excess reserves if they had any or borrowed from the Federal Reserve. From mid-1954 to December 1955, member banks increased their indebtedness to the Federal Reserve Banks by $700 million and reduced excess reserves by over $200 million. From mid-1958 to mid-1959 banks increased their borrowing at the Federal Reserve by $900 million, and again reduced their excess reserves by $200 million.

By late 1955 and again by mid-1959, many banks had borrowed virtually to the limit from their Federal Reserve Banks. These banks were the same ones which had drawn down their portfolios of short-term securities most heavily. They then found it necessary to become extremely selective in granting loans.

As we have already noted, banks had little difficulty in accommodating the loan demands of their customers during the early 1960's. The change in the ceiling rates made it possible for banks to bid for additional deposits whenever they needed them to accommodate loan demand.

When monetary policy turned to restraint in late 1965, it appeared for a time that banks could avoid the problems they had had in the tight-money periods of the previous decade. Loan demand was very strong in the first part of 1966 and the Federal Reserve was not increasing the reserve base. But banks were able to raise their rates on time deposits to attract additional funds. For a time they obliged their customers with little difficulty. But as market interest rates rose, banks found that the ceiling on time deposit interest rates limited their ability to attract more time deposits. With loan demand still rising, they quickly found themselves in the same kind of difficulties they had faced in the 1950's. The sudden change in credit conditions caused a near panic in the securities markets in the late summer of 1966 and played a significant part in checking the investment boom.

Federal Reserve policy turned toward ease in late 1966, and banks were again able to meet loan demand and to rebuild their security portfolios in 1967 and 1968. But with the return to a restrictive policy in 1969, the banks faced a new set of problems.

During the first half of 1969 the money supply grew at an annual rate of 5 per cent against 8 per cent in the previous year and during the second half of 1969, money supply growth was 2 per cent (at annual rate). As market interest rates rose, businesses replaced their certificates of deposits with marketable securities. With their time deposit rates held down by the regulation *Q* ceilings, banks found it difficult to accommodate the expanding loan demand from their customers. Demand deposits were growing slowly and the banks could not raise rates on time deposits. With interest rates rising, securities had to be sold at a loss. In these circumstances banks resorted to extraordinary measures to obtain funds—they borrowed from their foreign branches and issued commercial paper through affiliates.

In spite of the severe restraint imposed by the Federal Reserve, the large commercial banks were able to expand their business loans by over 10 per cent during 1969. But the intense competition for credit drove interest rates to the high levels previously cited. And although banks did manage to meet the bulk of their loan demand, they also tightened credit standards and refused loans that would have been granted in an easier money period.

THRIFT INSTITUTIONS

Until the late 1950's the mutual savings banks and the savings-and-loan associations were relatively unaffected by changes in monetary policy. Their rates were much higher than those offered by commercial banks and generally higher than those on short-term government securities. In 1959, however, the mutual savings banks suffered a significant amount of withdrawals by customers who were attracted by the high rates on government securities. In the early 1960's commercial banks increased their share of the savings market, but the other institutions also continued to grow rapidly.

In 1966, however, the thrift institutions suffered severely from competition with commercial banks and with marketable securities. The net inflow of funds to savings-and-loan associations and mutual savings banks dropped from $13 billion in 1965 to only $7 billion in 1966. The rate of inflow to the thrift institutions dropped off again in 1969. As Chapter 5 has shown, these shifts in the flow of funds had a very adverse effect on the rate of home building.

THE EFFECTS OF MONETARY POLICY

Did all these gyrations in monetary policy make any difference? Did the Federal Reserve control the economy, moderating but not determining its cyclical swings? Or was it just spinning its wheels?

The monetarist school regards the control by the Federal Reserve of the money supply as the dominant influence on the growth of demand. They give this institution all the credit and all the blame for the swings in employment and prices. Others (including most of the policy makers in the Federal Reserve System) think that Federal Reserve policy has a very substantial influence on the movement of demand. But they are willing to share the credit and the blame with fiscal policy makers, and they recognize that many other factors influence the economy.

The fact is that after more than 50 years of changing Federal Reserve policy, we're still not sure how monetary policy influences the economy.

Those who trace the impact of monetary policy through its effect on credit conditions—interest rates and credit availability—and then through the effect of changing credit conditions on spending, concur on the qualitative description of the impact of monetary policy. But they are not so certain about the quantities involved.

Everyone agrees that monetary policy has had a major impact on residential construction. The rate of residential construction has contracted in each tight-money period and expanded in each easy-money period. Expenditures on residential construction declined about $3 billion from 1955 to 1957 and again from 1959 to 1960. In 1966 they declined by $7 billion in less than a year. Such changes played a major role in slowing the growth of demand.

The accuracy of estimates of the effects of rising interest rates and credit rationing on business spending on plant and equipment is much less certain because so many factors are at work. But no one doubts that these factors have been significant.

The effect of monetary policy on consumption is still controversial. The easy monetary conditions of 1954 helped to trigger a sharp easing of consumer credit terms, which in turn contributed to the auto boom of 1955. Since then, cyclical changes in consumer credit terms have been very small. Some economists link consumption to changes in stock prices and continue this line of thinking by crediting monetary policy with a major influence on the stock market. The evidence on that point is not conclusive, although recent movements of the stock market and the savings rate tend to bear out the view.

In spite of the difficulty of measuring and predicting the impact of monetary policy, it is fair to say that, broadly speaking, Federal Reserve policy has worked to achieve the objective of checking the growth of demand during expansions and stimulating recovery from recessions.

There is, however, some question whether the more fundamental objective of moderating swings in business activity was achieved. Other forces, besides monetary policy, influenced the movement of demand, and monetary policy sometimes worked to offset their destabilizing effects but sometimes reinforced them.

Almost everyone agrees, for example, that the easy-money policy of 1953–1954 provided an important offset to the cutback in defense orders and expenditures after the Korean War. The rise in residential construction and the temporary stimulus to automobile demand helped to limit the recession and bring about the recovery of 1954–1955. Expansionary action in the other recessions was also clearly helpful.

In other cases, however, Federal Reserve policy may have applied the brakes to expansions that were already losing their momentum.

Many economists believe that the Federal Reserve kept the monetary brake on too long in 1957, thus contributing to the 1958 recession. And in view of the fiscal restraint in 1959, Federal Reserve policy was again too restrictive.

The war in Viet Nam has posed extremely difficult problems for the Federal Reserve, and it has made its share of mistakes. In particular, the light of hindsight shows that the effort to hold down interest rates in 1968 was a bad error. The Federal Reserve—and almost everyone else—underestimated the strength of inflationary forces and overestimated the impact of the tax surcharge. Their policy prolonged the inflation and necessitated the severely restrictive policy of 1969.

MONETARIST CRITICS

The monetarist critics of the Federal Reserve take an entirely different approach. They argue—following the new quantity theory outlined in Chapter 6—that the best measure of the effect of monetary policy on spending is the actual change in the money supply. They share with others the view that monetary policy was too easy in 1955 because the money supply was then growing at an unusually rapid rate. Some of them also agree with credit conditions analysts that money supply growth was too slow in the late phases of the 1954–1957 expansion. But the monetarists' criticism of the Federal Reserve's actions in recessions is far more severe. In the recessions of the 1950's the money supply declined or grew very slowly for several months after the recession had started. In these instances, there was no question of bad forecasting or excessive concern over inflation. The Federal Reserve, by its own account, was pursuing an easy-money policy while the money supply was lagging. The issue was not merely a question of the scale of action. Credit conditions analysts might agree that action to stimulate growth in money supply would have spurred the economy more. But in the monetarist view, the Federal Reserve was actually retarding the growth of demand by permitting a decline in the money supply.

As noted previously, those who take the credit conditions approach feel that erroneous forecasts led to some errors in Federal Reserve policy during the 1965–71 period. But the monetarists blame the Federal Reserve for all the instability of the past few years. In their view, the rapid expansion of the money supply in 1965 kicked off the inflation of 1966, the slow growth of money supply in 1966 led to the 1967 slow-down, and the expansion of money supply in 1967–1968 created new inflationary pressures. Finally, they blame the 1969 slow-down in monetary growth for causing the slow-down in economic activity in 1970.

LIMITS TO THE POWER OF MONETARY POLICY

Some people would like to rely on monetary policy as the primary instrument for controlling aggregate demand. They would like to see policy decisions that influence demand taken out of the political arena, leaving the management of aggregate demand to the central bank. They would like to find a way to separate decisions about taxes and expenditures from the short-run issues of unemployment and inflation. Fiscal orthodoxy in terms of an annually balanced budget, or at least a budget balanced at a full-employment level of income, would then be possible.

Can we rely on monetary policy to do the whole job of keeping the economy on an even keel? Monetary policy can do a good deal to offset variations in private investment demand, but it cannot do everything. For several years during the Great Depression of the 1930's credit conditions were as "easy" as possible. After 1934 interest rates fell to the lowest level in history, banks were almost completely out of debt, and member banks had huge amounts of excess reserves. Few people believe that more could have been done to make credit cheaper or more readily available.[2]

In spite of the very easy credit conditions existing from 1934 to 1940, however, private investment did not recover enough to produce full employment. "Hard cases make bad law." Certainly there were all sorts of peculiar circumstances during the 1930's. The experience does not demonstrate that monetary policy is a weak instrument; it only shows, unsurprisingly, that there is some limit to the powers of monetary policy. There is no reason to expect that there will always be enough private investment to absorb any volume of full-employment savings, even under the easiest monetary conditions. When private investment demand is weak, it may be necessary to use fiscal policy to reduce full-employment savings while we also use monetary policy to raise investment.

Monetary policy has its practical limits in the other direction, too. There is no doubt that, given sufficiently large open-market sales, the Federal Reserve could reduce investment by any amount that seemed advisable. But if the system had to act on too large a scale or too rapidly, its efforts at control might produce a financial panic.

Monetary policy is a powerful and useful instrument of economic policy, but it cannot solve all the problems of the economy.

SUMMARY

Federal Reserve policy has been directed toward assisting recovery from recessions by making credit easily and cheaply available. During the upswings of 1954–1957 and 1958–1960, monetary policy was aimed at restricting the rate of growth of demand to prevent further inflation. In the upswing beginning in 1961, unemployment remained high and prices stable

[2] Some writers contend that required reserves should not have been increased in 1937, insisting that the banks wanted the very large volume of excess reserves they held. And they argue that the increase in required reserves contributed substantially to the slump of 1938.

in spite of the growth of income over the next four years. Monetary policy was relatively easy during this period. It then was tightened considerably.

The course of monetary policy and its effects during recessions can be summarized as follows:

1. The Board of Governors and the Federal Open Market Committee recognize that a recession has begun or is impending.
2. Federal Reserve policy has three major instruments that can be used to ease credit conditions: (a) open-market purchases of securities, (b) reduction of the discount rate, (c) reduction of reserve requirements.

Of course, the monetary authorities do not do everything at once. As the recession proceeds, they take first one action then another to ease credit conditions. Their actions may be spread out over several months.

3. The banks respond to Federal Reserve actions through (a) repayment of debt to Federal Reserve banks, (b) purchases of securities and consequent increases in demand deposits, (c) increased willingness to lend.
4. Interest rates decline as a result of 3(b).
5. The flow of funds into savings and shares increases.
6. Costs are reduced and the availability of mortgage credit increases.
7. The rate of residential construction goes up.
8. Other types of investment expenditure increase as a consequence of lower interest rates and ready availability of bank loans.
9. Higher incomes and subsequent multiplier effects are observed.

During the upswings of 1954–1957 and 1958–1960, monetary events proceeded as follows:

1. Loan demand grew strongly during the upswing and banks sold large amounts of United States securities while increasing their loans.
2. Many banks with expanding loan demand had chronic difficulty in maintaining the reserve position required by law. Although they sold securities, they also borrowed from the Federal Reserve System.
3. The money supply expanded somewhat on the basis of borrowed reserves.
4. Increasing indebtedness to the Federal Reserve and the sale of holdings of short-term securities forced many banks to become more selective in granting loans.
5. The GNP rose faster than the money supply, and interest rates rose.
6. Rising interest rates reduced the rate of expenditure on residential construction.
7. Rising interest rates and bank credit rationing checked the expansion of other types of investment.

During the upswing beginning in 1961, monetary policy was relatively more expansionary.

1. Excess bank reserves exceeded bank borrowing of reserves until the end of 1964, as open-market operations provided the banks with additional reserves.
2. Loan demand grew substantially, but banks sold few government secur-

ities. Because of the extra reserves, they were able both to meet loan demands and to add to their investment holdings of state and local securities.

3. The money supply increased by about the same rate as real GNP, although less than GNP in current dollars.
4. Short-term interest rates rose gradually from 1961 to 1965, whereas long-term interest rates remained unchanged. The Federal Reserve sought to keep long-term rates low for domestic stimulus, leaving short-term rates high to keep short-term money from flowing out of the country and causing a gold drain.

During the period from 1965 to 1970 monetary policy makers faced a series of difficult decisions. A severely restrictive policy during 1966 helped to contain inflationary pressures but caused a sharp reduction in residential construction and endangered many financial institutions. During 1967–68 monetary policy was easier, but continuing inflationary pressures forced a return to a restrictive policy during 1969. In 1970 demand stopped growing, unemployment began to rise, and monetary policy again shifted toward ease.

During the period since 1945 monetary policy has demonstrated its power to influence the economy. But our experience indicates that monetary policy cannot control demand with any precision. Moreover, when demand is growing strongly, a restrictive monetary policy can have harmful effects on particular sectors of the economy and may endanger the stability of financial institutions.

Money and the Goals of Economic Policy

CHAPTER EIGHT

The experience of the last two decades has demonstrated that monetary policy can play an important role in controlling the level of national income and the rate of investment. But that very success has made the use of monetary policy a focus of controversy. The more effective a policy instrument, the more important it is to use it for the right objectives.

The Federal Reserve System has been concerned with four major objectives of economic policy: (1) full employment, (2) price stability, (3) economic growth, and (4) a satisfactory balance of payments. To some extent, measures taken to achieve one of those objectives assist in the achievement of others. But at times the different goals appear to be in conflict with one another. Can we have full employment and price stability at the same time? Do monetary measures required to maintain a satisfactory balance of payments lower the rate of growth? These questions have vexed economists and government officials for years and continue to do so.

We have already considered the impact of monetary policy on the level of income and employment. This chapter considers the influence of monetary policy on the price level, the rate of growth of potential output, and the balance of payments. We will note the points at which the different objectives of policy come into conflict, and we will mention some proposals for resolving the conflicts.

MONEY AND INFLATION

There is a long tradition of association between money and inflation. Many people assume that printing paper money or debasing a metallic coinage automatically leads to inflation. In discussions of the 1964 tax reduction, it has been argued that inflation would inevitably result if the government deficit were to be financed by an expansion of bank credit.

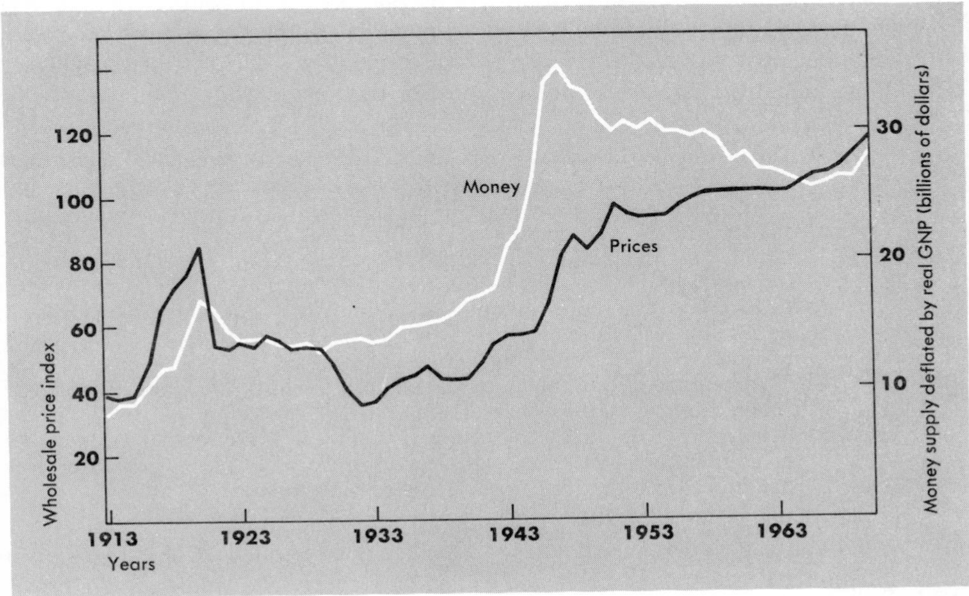

FIG. 8-1 Money supply (deflated by real GNP) and wholesale price index (Bureau of Labor Statistics), 1913–1970. (Sources: Prices—*Historical Statistics of the U.S.;* Money supply—*Federal Reserve Bulletin.*)

The most spectacular inflations have occurred during wars. Figure 8–1 shows that in those wartime inflations the quantity of money also increased faster than real output. Some economists regard this as evidence of a regular and simple connection between changes in the quantity of money and changes in prices. Other statistical evidence can be cited to support this view. The economists who emphasize the connection between money and prices uphold a modern version of the "quantity theory of money" mentioned in Chapter 6. But outside of the wartime periods, the connection between changes in money supply and changes in prices is not so strong or obvious. Most economists agree that there is a connection between changes in money supply and changes in prices, but they see it as an indirect one: (1) the money supply influences expenditures for goods and services and (2) the rate of expenditure for goods and services influences the movement of prices.

We have already considered the influence of money on GNP. Let us now turn to the link between GNP and prices.

GNP and Prices

There is a connection between the growth of GNP expenditures, the growth of potential output, and changes in the price level. *If* the growth of expenditures resulting from an increased money supply or any other factor tends to outrun the growth of potential output, prices will tend to rise. As long as demand falls substantially short of potential output, the effect on prices may be slight; but as the amount of unused resources narrows, prices will rise more quickly. There are several reasons for this relationship.

1. Employment will rise as output increases; unemployment will shrink and shortages of labor may develop in some labor markets even though unemployment exists elsewhere. Wages will tend to rise more rapidly.
2. Profits will rise and employers will find it easier to grant wage increases.
3. A reduction in unemployment will strengthen the bargaining position of unions.
4. Capacity will be more fully utilized. Competition for additional sales will be less intense. Business firms will find it easy to raise prices and profit margins and to "pass on" wage increases.
5. The resulting rise in the cost of living will intensify the wage demands of union members and other workers as well.
6. Moreover, once prices have been rising for a while, employers will become more confident that wage increases can be offset by price increases and will therefore grant wage increases more readily.

The last two points have two significant consequences. First, once an inflation has started, price increases tend to accelerate, and second, prices will continue to rise for a considerable length of time after demand pressures have relaxed and unemployment has risen.

Full Employment with Price Stability?

The considerations just stated lead to two conclusions. The rate of wage and price increase will be higher at low levels of unemployment than at higher levels, for one thing. Furthermore, the full effects of a change in the level of unemployment will not be felt at once. When the level of unemployment falls, the rate of price increase will rise fairly quickly, but it will continue to rise for some time even if there is no further decline in unemployment. And prices will continue to rise for some time even after demand pressures have relaxed and unemployment has risen.

These points are illustrated by the data in Fig. 8–2. You can see at a glance that prices have risen more rapidly in the years when unemployment was relatively low than in those when it was higher. But notice also how much

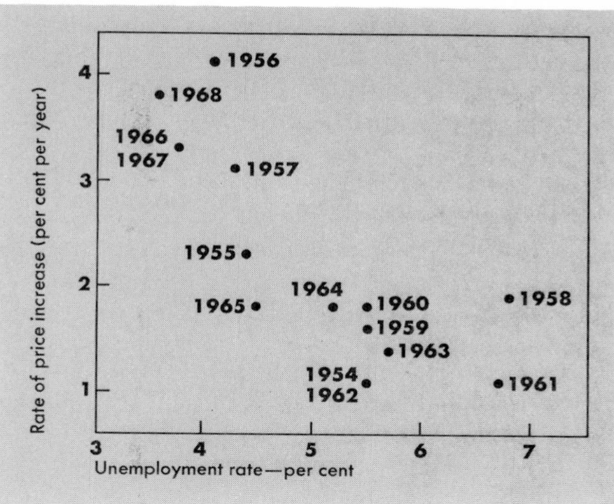

FIG. 8-2 Price performance and unemployment. (Source: *Council of Economic Advisers Report to the President*, February, 1969.)

more prices increased in 1969 than in 1968, although the unemployment rate was unchanged. And notice how much more prices increased in 1970, after several years of inflation, than in other years with 5 per cent unemployment.

The record of unemployment and price changes shows the dilemma with which policy makers have been wrestling for the last 25 years. "Full employment" has been accepted as a goal of public policy, and a 4 per cent unemployment rate has been widely accepted as a satisfactory definition of full employment. At the same time, price stability is also a goal of public policy. Yet the record indicates that when unemployment was as low as 4 per cent prices tended to rise at 3 to 5 per cent. Worse yet, the rate of price increase tends to accelerate when unemployment is relatively low. Even if we were willing to accept a 5 per cent rate of price increase to achieve "full employment," we might find that sustained full employment would lead to continuously accelerating price increases. Unfortunately, since we have only managed to maintain low rates of unemployment for relatively brief periods, we do not know what would happen if we really achieved sustained full employment.

This state of affairs poses a "Do you still beat your wife?" kind of question to policy makers. A fiscal and monetary policy aimed at price stability will lead to too much unemployment; policies aimed at full employment will result in an unacceptable rate of inflation; and a compromise will produce criticism for both sides.

But having to choose between inflation or unemployment puts the monetary authorities in an unenviable—and unfair—situation. The challenge to economic policy as a whole is to ease this choice, to work to reconcile these objectives. We can try to improve our labor markets—retraining displaced workers, improving the efficiency of the United States Employment Service, assisting workers to migrate from depressed areas, and so on. And we can try to make collective bargaining reflect the national interest in stability of costs; we can try to persuade leaders of industry who have some price-setting discretion to give full weight to the national interest in price stability.

Currently a variety of "incomes policies" aimed at restraining wage and price increases are under discussion. Certainly there are lots of things to be tried before we decide that we must make the choice between too much unemployment or too much inflation.

MONETARY POLICY AND THE BALANCE OF PAYMENTS

Until recently, decisions about monetary and fiscal policy have turned entirely on domestic issues. We have been fortunate in our ability to neglect balance-of-payments problems in making our choices. But we are an important international trading nation. And the dollar is an international reserve currency. Many countries hold reserves in the form of dollar bank balances or short-term United States securities.

The United States has sold more goods and services than it has bought abroad for many years. But we have also made large foreign investments, paying for foreign securities with dollars. And American firms have been building plants abroad and paying for them with dollars. In addition we have heavy military expenditures abroad, and we expend $3 billion a year in foreign aid.

Every time an American buys foreign goods or uses foreign services we pay dollars to foreigners. When we buy securities or make military expenditures abroad, we pay dollars to foreigners. We don't ship them dollar bills, however; Americans write checks on their bank balances and the credit on the books of an American bank is given to foreigners. Most foreign individuals or businessmen who receive dollar balances sell them to their own central banks for their home currency. Foreign central banks then sell dollars to their own citizens who have to make payments in the United States. When foreigners buy goods and services in the United States, the ownership of balances in American banks is transferred back to United States citizens.

If in some particular year we pay foreigners more than they pay us, they realize a net increase in their holdings of dollars. The amount of that net increase is called the balance-of-payments deficit of the United States. Until 1971, foreign central banks could exchange part of their dollar bank balances for gold by giving the Treasury a check. So the balance-of-payments deficit is the sum of (1) the increase in foreign holdings of dollars and (2) our sales of gold to foreign central banks. The balance-of-payments deficit is also the excess of all United States payments to foreigners over all their payments to us.

The United States has had a balance-of-payments deficit in most years since the end of World War II. The deficit averaged $1 billion per year from

1951 through 1957. But in 1958 the deficit rose to $3.5 billion and, although fluctuating, has averaged over $3 billion per year in the period from 1958 to 1964. The deficits declined in 1965 and 1966 but rose again in the late 1960's.

The continuing deficit in the balance of payments was reflected in a rise in foreign holdings of dollars and a decline in the U.S. gold stock. In 1948 our gold stock stood at $24.4 billion and foreign dollar balances at $6.1 billion. By 1969 our gold stock was less than $12 billion and foreign holdings of dollars had risen to over $28 billion. The continuing decline in gold reserves and the rise in claims against them caused apprehension about the ability of the U.S. to maintain the international value of the dollar.

There has been much dispute over the causes of our balance-of-payments deficit. Some have attributed the difficulty to inflation. "We have priced ourselves out of the market," is a frequent comment. In most of the post-World War II period, however, U.S. consumer prices have risen more slowly than those in other industrial countries. But the prices of the goods we export have risen somewhat faster than the export prices of our major trading rivals. Prices of American exports rose relatively fast in the late 1950's and again in the late 1960's after the expansion of the war in Viet Nam. Our share of world exports of manufactured goods has declined, particularly in the fields of steel and machinery.

Our exports have been held down by factors other than prices, too. Some of our best customers (e.g., Latin America) have been developing slowly. The development of the European Common Market and the increasing importance of quotas and other nontariff barriers to trade also affect our competitive position.

In spite of some loss in our share of world markets, we usually sell more abroad than we buy. But the balance of payments includes other things besides commercial exports and imports. The war in Viet Nam has had a significant adverse effect on our balance of payments, and our military expenditures in Europe are also costly in balance-of-payments terms. In spite of our efforts to "tie" foreign aid to exports from the U.S., our foreign aid expenditures tend to increase our balance-of-payments deficit. Some people believe we should decrease these expenditures. Such cuts would not improve our payments dollar-for-dollar, however, because many of our commercial exports result from our aid programs.

Our balance of payments is also affected by a huge volume of international capital transactions. Around 1958 the Western European currencies became freely convertible into other currencies. American lenders began to consider it safe to lend in Europe and Japan. Since interest rates in the U.S. were lower than in other countries, there was a rapid increase in foreign security sales in this country. In addition, foreigners found it easier to borrow in the U.S. because the money market here is larger and better organized than any other. It is easier to borrow a large sum in New York than anywhere else in the world. The convertibility of European currencies and the development of the Common Market encouraged American manufacturers to expand their production facilities abroad. Each year American firms spend several billion dollars on acquiring new overseas facilities. Since American firms have been investing abroad for many years, there is a very large return flow of interest and dividends from past investments. Moreover, much of the direct business investment by American firms is financed by borrowing in Europe. In that case, U.S. direct investment abroad has no adverse affect on the balance of payments.

Capital flows are not, of course, a one-way street. When U.S. interest rates are relatively high, as in 1969, American businesses and banks borrow large sums from Europeans. And Europeans have been increasingly attracted by the opportunity for investment in common stocks of American companies.

The Dollar as a World Currency

The position of the U.S. is unique because the dollar is a reserve currency. Any other country must sooner or later find a way to eliminate a balance-of-payments deficit because it will eventually run out of reserves. But so long as other countries have confidence that the real value of the dollar will not decline relative to the real value of other currencies, the U.S. can run a moderate deficit every year for many years. The dollar is the currency used for international payments throughout the noncommunist world. The increase in the volume of trade generates a steady increase in the amount of dollars needed for transactions purposes by foreign businesses and banks. And since there are only limited supplies of other reserves (gold and International Monetary Fund Special Drawing Rights) foreign central banks are willing to add to their stocks of dollars each year.

Because the dollar is a reserve currency, it can have deficits every year provided (1) the deficits are not so large that foreign central banks acquire large amounts of *unwanted* dollar reserves and (2) the U.S. price performance is comparatively good. In some respects the U.S. is in the position of a bank. It can pay for earning assets—foreign securities and direct investments with dollar balances (and short-term securities at relatively low interest rates)—because foreigners need those short-term dollar assets for reserve and for transactions purposes.

Balance-of-Payments Policy

The basic logic of balance-of-payments policy for nonreserve countries is fairly simple. The remedy for a persisting balance-of-payments deficit or surplus should be suited to the cause. A country may sometimes be satisfied with its domestic situation in terms of rate of inflation and level of unemployment and still find that it has a balance-of-payments surplus or deficit. The surplus or deficit may arise because of events elsewhere or because of the country's military expenditures, its foreign aid, or its investment policies. If there is no good domestic reason to change policy, the remedy for a nonreserve country is to change the value of its currency in terms of the dollar (and other currencies as well). A surplus country should raise the value of its currency, a deficit country should lower it.

On the other hand, if the balance-of-payments difficulty arises from policies that are regarded as wrong from a domestic point of view, then obviously those policies should be corrected, and the change will also improve the balance-of-payments situation. (Sometimes a devaluation will be required anyway to offset the adverse effects of the inflation that has taken place before the change in domestic policy.)

Traditionally, countries faced with balance-of-payments problems have used monetary policy as a means of eliminating their deficits. The Bank of England has raised its discount rate to 7 per cent in balance-of-payments crises. A restrictive monetary policy tends to reduce a country's balance-of-payments deficit in three ways: (1) It tends to reduce demand in the country applying it, which in turn tends to reduce the demand for imports as well as for domestic products. (2) The reduction in domestic demand holds down the rate of inflation or reduces prices, which makes imported goods less attractive to the country's citizens and makes the deficit country's exports more attractive to foreigners. (3) Higher interest rates make it less attractive for foreigners to borrow in the deficit country and more attractive for them to invest there.

The United States is in a somewhat different situation. It probably should run a significant deficit most of the time to meet the world demand for dollars. But when an inflation that is undesirable at home causes an excessive balance-of-payments deficit, the country should take measures to restrict the growth of demand.

But what if domestic demand is not excessive or, as in the early 1960's actually deficient, and we still have too large a balance-of-payments deficit? We cannot follow the rules for a nonreserve country and devalue. We could change the price of gold but that would not, in itself, alter the value of other currencies in terms of the dollar. We would have to sit tight and wait for the countries with surpluses (matching the U.S. deficits) to raise the value of their currencies relative to the dollar, as the West Germans did in 1969. Unfortunately exchange rate adjustments are a political issue in every country and do not occur in any automatic way.

At present, most economists believe that the U.S. should pursue a "passive" balance-of-payments policy. That is, we should do what we think is right from a domestic point of view. If other countries accumulate more dollars than they want, it is for *them* to take action by raising the value of their currencies. If such a policy is feasible, there will be no conflict between balance-of-payments and domestic-policy objectives. But although passivity may be a basically sound balance-of-payments policy, a large balance-of-payments deficit will always enter as a factor weighting the scales toward high interest rates and restrictive monetary policy in every dispute over the correct domestic policy.

In the years since balance-of-payments deficits became significant, the U.S. government has adopted a number of measures to improve the balance of payments. These include a drive to attract tourists and a variety of measures to increase exports, requirements that foreign aid grants and loans be spent in the United States, and the sale of American military equipment to some of our European allies. In the monetary field, the Federal Reserve and the Treasury raised short-term interest rates to discourage lending abroad while at the same time holding down long-term rates in the period 1961–1965. In 1964 an interest equalization tax was levied on foreign securities issued in the U.S., designed to raise the interest cost to foreigners by 1 per cent a year. In 1965 a voluntary program of restraint on investment abroad by corporations was initiated, and the Federal Reserve asked banks to limit their increase of bank loans abroad. These controls were strengthened in 1968.

The measures adopted had some success—in particular, the restraints on dollar outflows for direct investment have induced American firms to finance their foreign plants by borrowing in Europe. But they were not sufficient to offset the deterioration in the U.S. trade balance caused by the inflation after 1966. In the first half of 1971 the United States had its first trade deficit since 1893. The announcement of the trade deficit and the persistence of inflation in the face of continuing unemployment led to a wave of speculation against the dollar.

In response, the President announced that the Treasury would no longer sell gold to foreign central banks. At the same time, he imposed a 10 per cent surcharge on dutiable imports and, by executive order, froze all wages and prices.

The suspension of gold convertibility and the import surcharge were emergency measures. The first measure put other nations on notice that they would have to either accumulate dollars or adjust their exchange rates. The second provided a bargaining counter to encourage exchange rate adjustments. A new system of international coordination of exchange rates will eventually emerge, but it will take some time before it takes shape. The price freeze was also an interim measure designed to prevent price increases, pending the development of a more permanent incomes policy.

MONETARY POLICY, FISCAL POLICY, AND RESOURCE ALLOCATION

Monetary policy and fiscal policy are both instruments for controlling total demand. But they affect the aggregate through their impact on specific components of demand. Government expenditures and taxes have a visible and direct effect on specific sectors of the economy. The effects of monetary policy are concentrated on specific sectors even though they are indirect.

Monetary policy influences capital spending through its effect on the cost and availability of credit. To the extent that plant and equipment spending is checked by a restrictive monetary policy, future growth is restricted. But on the record, it appears that the housing sector sustains more damage due to restrictive monetary policy than any other type of capital formation. In spite of the development of agencies like the Federal National Mortgage Agency and the Federal Home Loan Banks, housing still remains vulnerable to restrictive monetary policy. Indeed, because it uses so much more borrowed capital than any other sector, it is almost inevitable that housing construction will be seriously affected by any policy that draws *open* interest rates.

A high rate of residential construction is in itself an object of social policy, so that monetary policy makers often find themselves faced with another conflict of objectives. If a restrictive monetary policy appears necessary in order to achieve some GNP target (chosen after consideration of the inflation–unemployment problem), policy makers find themselves forced either to permit an unsuitably large increase in price or to unduly restrict housing demand. That dilemma can be avoided by an appropriate fiscal policy. More precisely, the full-employment rate of saving should be high enough to equal the full-employment rate of investment generated by the monetary conditions we desire. If we want easy money to foster growth, we must be willing to pay the price by saving enough to provide for the investment we want.

Notice, however, that the combination of fiscal and monetary policy suitable for encouraging investment (i.e., tight fiscal policy and easy money) is precisely the opposite of the one suggested for solving the balance-of-payments problem.

SUMMARY

The goals of economic policy include (1) full employment, (2) stable prices, (3) a high rate of growth, and (4) a satisfactory balance-of-payments position. Monetary policy influences the level of employment, the price level, the rate of growth, and the balance of payments. The level of employment is influenced by the level of interest rates and the availability of credit. The rate of increase of prices tends to rise as we approach full employment. Notice that monetary policy influences prices through its influence on employment and capacity utilization. An effort to control inflation by monetary action tends to increase unemployment simultaneously.

Monetary policy influences the balance of payments because low interest rates at home encourage Americans to invest abroad and encourage foreigners to hold their short-term balances outside the U.S.

Low interest rates tend to increase the rate of investment in plant and equipment in this country and so increase the rate of growth of potential output.

In making monetary policy, it is often necessary to choose among conflicting objectives. The conflicts among objectives may be reduced by the use of other policies. Thus the rate of inflation at full employment can be reduced by a variety of measures to improve the operation of our labor markets.

We saw in Chapter 6 that various combinations of monetary policy and fiscal policy are consistent with full employment. Thus an easy-money policy can be used to foster a high rate of capital formation provided that fiscal policy is used to provide a sufficiently high level of full employment saving.

Selected Readings

For detailed treatments of money and banking, any of the following intermediate textbooks are recommended: Eli Shapiro et al., *Money and Banking,* 5th ed. (New York: Holt, Rinehart & Winston, 1968); Lester Chandler, *The Economics of Money and Banking,* 5th ed. (New York: Harper, 1969); George N. Halm, *Economics of Money and Banking* (Homewood, Ill.: Irwin, 1961); Albert B. Hart and Peter B. Kenen, *Money, Debt and Economic Activity,* 5th ed. (Englewood Cliffs, N.J.: Prentice-Hall, 1969); A. C. L. Day and Sterie T. Beza, *Money and Income* (New York: Oxford University Press, 1960); and Dennis H. Robertson, *Money* (Chicago: University of Chicago Press, 1959).

For readings in a wide variety of topics in money and banking, see Lawrence S. Ritter, *Money and Economic Activity,* 2nd ed. (Boston: Houghton Mifflin, 1961); and James A. Crutchfield et al., *Money, Financial Institutions and the Economy* (Englewood Cliffs, N.J.: Prentice-Hall, 1965).

On the origins and development of money, see Paul Einzig, *Primitive Money in Its Ethnological, Historical and Economic Aspects* (New York: Humanities Press). A succinct account of American banking history is provided by Bray Hammond, "Historical Introduction," in *Banking Studies,* Board of Governors of the Federal Reserve System, Washington, D.C.: 1941.

On the organization of the Federal Reserve System, see *The Federal Reserve System: Its Structure and Function,* 4th ed., Board of Governors of the Federal Reserve System, Washington, D.C.: 1961. The conduct of open-market operations is described in R. V. Roosa, *Federal Reserve Operations in the Money and Securities Markets,* Federal Reserve Bank of New York, New York, 1956.

For a more detailed analysis of bank management problems, see Roland Robinson, *Management of Bank Funds,* 2nd ed. (New York: McGraw-Hill, 1962). An interesting picture of day-to-day reserve management problems is given in *The Money Side of the Streets,* Federal Reserve Bank of New York.

The Commission on Money and Credit has published a series of volumes covering the history, functions, and problems of public regulation of the major financial institutions, all published by Prentice-Hall, Inc., Englewood Cliffs, N.J., 1963. Following are the titles: *The Commercial Banking Industry; The Consumer Finance Industry; Life Insurance Companies as Financial Institutions; Management Investment Companies; Mortgage Companies; Mutual Savings Banking; Property and Casualty Insurance Companies; The Savings and Loan Business; Federal Credit Agencies; Federal Credit Programs; Private Capital Markets;* and *Private Financial Institutions.*

For a theoretical view of the role of financial intermediaries, see Edward S. Shaw and John G. Gurley, *Money In a Theory of Finance* (Washington, D.C.: The Brookings Institution, 1960). For an overall view of capital markets, see H. E. Dougall, *Capital Markets and Institutions* (Englewood Cliffs, N.J.: Prentice-Hall, 1970).

The problems of Federal Reserve policy in the early post-World War II years were thoroughly aired in two sets of congressional hearings. See U.S. Congress, Joint Committee on the Economic Report, Subcommittee on Monetary Credit and Fiscal Policy, *Hearing,* 1949, *Statements,* 1949, *Report,* 1950, 81st Congress (commonly called the Douglas Committee Report); and U.S. Congress Joint Economic Committee, Subcommittee on General Credit Control and Debt Management, *Hearings, Replies to Questions and Other Material. Report,* 82nd Congress, 2nd Session, 1952 (Patman Committee). More recent developments are reviewed in G. L. Bach, *Making Monetary and Fiscal Policy* (Washington, D.C.: The Brookings Institution, 1971). Also see *Controlling Monetary Aggregates,* Federal Reserve Bank of Boston, 1970.

For a radical critique of all our money institutions, see Milton Friedman, *Program for Monetary Stability* (New York: Fordham University Press, 1959). On the supply of money and changes in prices and output, see Milton Friedman and Anna Schwartz, *A Monetary History of the United States, 1867-1960* (Princeton: Princeton University Press, 1963).

Most of the issues in monetary policy are viewed in the Report of the Commission on Money and Credit. A comprehensive source of data is the *Federal Reserve Bulletin,* a monthly publication of the Federal Reserve Board.

Index

Index